# WEYMOUTH
## CENTURY

Maureen Attwooll and Colin A. Pomeroy

DORSET BOOKS

First published in Great Britain in 2003
Reprinted 2004

British Library Cataloguing-in-Publication Data
**A CIP record for this title is available from the British Library**


ISBN 1 871164 42 7


**DORSET BOOKS**
Official Publisher to Dorset County Council

Halsgrove House
Lower Moor Way
Tiverton EX16 6SS
T: 01884 243242
F: 01884 243325

sales@halsgrove.com
www.halsgrove.com


Printed and bound in Great Britain
by CPI Bath

# CONTENTS

# ACKNOWLEDGEMENTS

The majority of the old photographs in *Weymouth Century* are from Weymouth Library's Local Studies Collection, amongst which are a number from the Graham Herbert collection. We thank the library staff for their help and co-operation. Transport historian Brian Jackson advised us on road and rail topics and provided us with pictures of Colwell House, the landslip on the Weymouth and Portland Railway and Woodhouse's shop in St Thomas Street. Colin Caddy allowed us to use his photographs of Littlefield Level Crossing, Lower Bond Street, Overcombe and Radipole Spa Bus Garage. Jim Smith took the photograph of the Health Centre and Joe Ward photographed the Railway Dock Hotel. Joe Ward also allowed us to reproduce the illustration of King George VI at Weymouth Pier in 1938 which is in his collection. David Gordon-Steward lent us a rare picture of Nottington House. David Attwooll photographed the storm-damaged stone pier; the pictures of Belfield House, Cosens' Cold Store and the old Weymouth Museum were taken by Jack West. The family of the late Eric Ricketts kindly gave us permission to use his drawings of Belfield House and the Congregational Chapel in West Street. The pictures of the Municipal Offices at night and the demolition of Sunnybank electricity power station are by Bill Macey. Head Teacher John Horrell of St John's School supplied the photograph of the school in Coombe Avenue and Captain Mike Roughton lent us the photograph of the helicopter G-BPWB. The picture of the Maiden Street Methodist Church fire was supplied by the *Dorset Echo* and Ron Martin provided the picture of the bomb-damaged houses in Franchise Street. Weymouth Museum lent us the picture of G-EBLA at Lodmoor Airfield, Robert Bowditch provided the photograph of Littlemoor Road Junction, David Chambers photographed the Weymouth Harbour ferryman and Tony Gregson provided us with a current street map. We thank all of these contributors for their very willing help and generosity. Other pictures used are from the authors' own collections. If we have inadvertently used a picture without due acknowledgement, we offer our sincere apologies – for we have tried to ascertain the original ownership of all the photographs. Finally, our thanks are due to our publishers, Dorset Books, for their help and encouragement during the project – and to our respective spouses, David and Binks, who have patiently put up with our absence from home as we meandered around the town and then spent hours at the computer. Any mistakes in the book are, of course, entirely our own.

# INTRODUCTION

**W**eymouth *Century* combines images of the town at the start of the twenty-first century with those of an earlier age. We have selected more than seventy old local scenes and photographed the same view in 2003 – pictures taken, wherever possible, from the same vantage point as the earlier photographers.

We hope that the collection of illustrations in the book will evoke memories for long-time residents of the Weymouth area and introduce newer Weymouthians and visitors to aspects of the town and its development over the past one hundred years or so which are not immediately recognisable today. As we made our various expeditions to photograph the modern views – taking with us of course the old illustrations that we were aiming to reproduce – interest in the project was lively and rewarding. We frequently gathered a small group around us, poring over the old pictures whilst exchanging reminiscences and memories of times past – the stuff of which local history is made! The additional photographs which appear in the text provide links both old and new to the main illustrations.

Our thanks are recorded on the previous page to people who generously lent pictures for inclusion in *Weymouth Century*, but we must also acknowledge the help of those who contributed when we were 'out and about'. Some were good enough to let us into their properties so that we could take pictures from windows at first- and second-floor level; others very kindly moved their vehicles a few feet so that a car or taxi did not become the focal point of our photograph – vehicles and the parking of them presenting very real problems as we endeavoured to capture a street scene in 2003. It is a curious anomaly that an old photograph is so much more interesting when it shows the transport of yesteryear – be it a horse and carriage, a charabanc or even a 1950s Vauxhall Velox motor car – yet a row of modern saloons or people-carriers does little to enhance today's scene. Perhaps fifty years from now future advances in transport technology will be the cause of nostalgic reminiscing when a Volkswagen Golf or a Mitsubishi Shogun is spotted in an old photograph of Weymouth.

Our choice of the 'Then' illustrations in this 'Then and Now' collection has been made mainly from photographs taken after 1900, but we have occasionally strayed back into the nineteenth century if the view is of particular interest. The quality of many of the early pictures is superb and it is a great shame that we cannot credit the original photographers, for the majority of the prints that we have used bear no name on the reverse and few are dated, hence some of our dates are approximate.

We sincerely hope that *Weymouth Century* will not only provide a link with the past, but also provide an impetus to ensure that what remains will be enjoyed and appreciated by future generations.

# Alexandra Gardens

*Alexandra Gardens, c.1913*

Located at the southern end of Weymouth Esplanade, the Alexandra Gardens were laid out on land purchased for the town in the 1860s by George Robert Stephenson, a wealthy yacht-owning visitor to Weymouth. The gardens were named after Princess Alexandra, the popular 'Alix', bride of the Prince of Wales, later King Edward VII. The area had previously been known as 'The Rings', a series of grassy spaces enclosed by railings, and early prints show animals grazing here. Bandstands were the first entertainment feature in the grounds and they were followed in 1913 by this glass structure known as the Kursaal. It was built around the former open-air bandstand, the roof of which can be seen in its centre. The high roof behind it is that of the Marine Hotel, better remembered in recent years as the Edward Hotel, and which has now been converted to apartments. During the First World War the Kursaal served as a reception centre for hundreds of wounded Australian soldiers – men injured, many very seriously, in the fighting at Gallipoli and later in France. The troops were sent to treatment and convalescence camps set up at Littlemoor, Westham, Chickerell and Portland. The Australian street names in some parts of the borough, such as Sydney Street, Queensland Road and Canberra Crescent, recall these antipodean visitors. The Kursaal lasted just over ten years. It was replaced in 1924 by the Alexandra Concert Hall, later to be known as the Alexandra Gardens Theatre.

*Alexandra Gardens, 2003*

In 2003 this amusements complex has replaced the theatre of 1924. Until the early 1960s the theatre was a popular venue for both seaside summer shows and plays performed by touring theatrical companies, but competition from its new neighbour the Pavilion Theatre and the attractions of television brought about its closure. In 1964 the Alexandra Gardens Theatre was converted to an amusements centre. Fire destroyed the building in September 1993, and this photograph shows the rebuilt amusements which now stand on the site. The roof of the former Edward Hotel is just visible in the centre background of the picture.

*Open-air brass band concerts were once a very popular feature of seaside holidays. This attractive bandstand stood in the Alexandra Gardens from 1891 until 1924, when it was removed to the Nothe Gardens. Sadly, it was removed from there, too, in the 1960s and Weymouth no longer has an outdoor concert venue.*

*When the present Pavilion Theatre was built in 1960, the Clark and Endicott Memorial, which had formerly been located in front of the old theatre, was removed to a position in the Alexandra Gardens where it stayed for more than forty years. The monument commemorates two men whose voyages in the sixteenth and seventeenth centuries began in the port of Weymouth: Richard Clark set out in 1583 to accompany Sir Humphrey Gilbert's expedition to Newfoundland and John Endicott left in 1628 for America, to become one of the founders – and later Governor – of the State of Massachusetts. Restored by Weymouth College's Stone Masonry Department, the monument was unveiled at a new site beside the ferry steps near the Pavilion Theatre on 8 March 2003. Nearby, Weymouth Civic Society has placed a bench seat of Portland Stone in memory of its late President Eric Ricketts, who died in October 2002 – noted architect, historian and author of a series of invaluable books on the borough's history.*

# Belfield House

*Belfield House, 1825*

John William Upham was a local schoolteacher who painted many scenes in and around Weymouth in the early nineteenth century. This is his view of one of Weymouth's finest buildings – Belfield House. It is sited now in Belfield Park Avenue but, as Upham's engraving clearly shows, it was once surrounded by magnificent parkland. This filled the whole of the area between Buxton Road and Wyke Road and extended as far as today's Cross Road which links the two main roads. Noted architect John Crunden designed Belfield around 1780 for Isaac Buxton, after whom the road is named, although in his day it was merely Buxton's Lane. A wealthy merchant and Member of Parliament, Buxton was an active campaigner in William Wilberforce's anti-slavery lobby. King George III's family visited Belfield when holidaying at Weymouth. In Victorian times some land was sold off to build 'Portmore', a rectory for the wealthy incumbent of St Mary's Church. 'Portmore' (since demolished) is better remembered by its later name 'Connaught House', and many Weymouth children of the late 1940s, 1950s and 1960s attended classes there as a temporary measure to ease overcrowding in their own schools.

*Belfield House, 1974*

Much more of Belfield's park was sold in the twentieth century. The houses which now surround the mansion and trees which screen it from the road prevented a suitable 2003 view of the front of the house to compare with Upham's engraving. This photograph was taken in the 1970s and the row of cypresses in front of Belfield has now grown almost to the height of the house.

*Not far from Belfield a long lane leads down to the sea from Buxton Road and almost a century ago Rylands Lane really was a country lane with high hedges on either side. This early-1900s view looks north towards its junction with Buxton Road, and the Edwardian families appear to be on a blackberrying expedition. Although today this is a busy urban road with houses along its length, Rylands Lane well within living memory was noted for its unmade surface and enormous potholes which made cycling and driving a somewhat hazardous undertaking.*

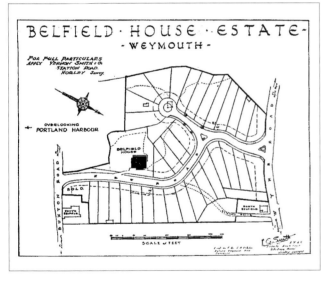

*This plan shows not only the plots of land around Belfield House which were for sale in 1933, but also the extent of the parkland. The new road (later named Belfield Park Avenue, with Belfield Park Drive leading off it) cut right across the parkland between Buxton Road and Wyke Road. It was from Wyke Road that the original main drive had led down to the house. Off Buxton Road was South Belfield, once the coach house and stable block but since converted to housing. Buxton Close and Belfield Close, directly opposite the house, were later developments and do not appear on the plan. The photograph opposite was taken from Buxton Close.*

*Although no longer encircled by the beautiful grounds of yesteryear, the house still retains the elegance of the Georgian era. The sketch is by Eric Ricketts.*

# Broadwey

*Broadwey, c.1925*

This was the old farmhouse at Broadwey around 1925. It stands some 100 yards south of St Nicholas Church (not to be confused with St Nicholas Church in Buxton Road) and is now No 625 Dorchester Road. The oldest part of the farm, the low section farthest from the camera, dates from the late seventeenth century. Dorchester Road was rather less hazardous for pedestrians in the twenties. Imagine the dangers of stepping out past the farm buildings today if there was no pavement in front of them, as here!

*Broadwey, 2003*

The farm ceased to operate in the early 1950s and the old farmhouse is now a sympathetically restored dwelling house, its thatch replaced by roof tiles and its bay windows removed. South of the farm was its barn, also now converted to a house. Heavy traffic on Dorchester Road is subject to frequent delays and the merits of various costly relief road schemes to bypass it (the Orange, Purple and Brown Routes) have been under discussion for years without any real advancement.

*Just north of the old Broadwey farmhouse, on the east side of Dorchester Road and opposite the church, was the village school. It was extended several times in the late-nineteenth and early-twentieth centuries but this early photograph probably shows it as first built in the 1830s, its rural setting much changed today. Since 1972 the children of Broadwey have attended St Nicholas and St Laurence Church of England Primary School, along with Upwey youngsters whose Victorian village school closed in 1976. The old Broadwey School buildings have been converted to houses.*

*Close to both Broadwey's old farmhouse and school is the former railway station building on the Abbotsbury branch line, named, slightly confusingly, 'Upwey Station'. The attractive stone-built station building survives, but it is now surrounded by the stores and offices of the small commercial estate which has grown up on the site. The Abbotsbury line closed in December 1952, but Upwey Station, renamed 'Upwey Goods', remained in use until the 1960s. The 'Old Station Yard' turning off Dorchester Road is just north of St Nicholas Church.*

# Brunswick Terrace

*Brunswick Terrace, c.1900*

Brunswick Terrace, once known as Brunswick Buildings, was built at the northern end of the Esplanade and its houses are the first to actually stand on the promenade, unlike the Esplanade terraces further south which are separated from it by a busy roadway.  Built in the 1820s, the row of 20 bow-windowed houses had changed little in the sixty or so years before this photograph was taken. The rather more ornate façade of the house in the foreground is one of a slightly later pair added to the end of the original terrace. The little shelter which stood on the shingle was removed when the prom here was widened in the 1920s.

*Brunswick Terrace, 2003*

In 2003 the railings fronting these properties have gone and most have patio areas adjacent to the pavement. The road which runs along the front of Brunswick Terrace has no exit for traffic at its northern end, and since the completion of the sea defence works and new Preston Beach wall in 1995 it has been possible to walk along the Esplanade all the way to Overcombe. Shop-style windows have replaced the ground-floor bows of one or two of the properties, but the terrace is largely unspoilt. The Esplanade section of the 1930s Pier Bandstand is in the background.

*A scene from around 1900, looking towards Brunswick Terrace. At this exposed spot a shelter or tent has been set up, for the musicians who provided outdoor brass band concerts which were popular features in the seaside resorts.*

*This bandstand is of the early 1900s. A more permanent structure, it stood on the shingle just south of Brunswick Terrace. As can be seen, this became quite a congested spot when strollers paused to listen to the day's concert, and later in the twentieth century the Esplanade would be extended out around the bandstand. The Pier Bandstand replaced this little outdoor music venue in 1939.*

*This was the winning design in a competition held to select a successor to the Edwardian bandstand. The crowd has turned out to watch the official opening of the Pier Bandstand in May 1939. Local opinion was divided over the merits of the Pier Bandstand but many enjoyed the events held there its 1950s heyday – the evening open-air dances, Miss Weymouth contests, wrestling, roller-skating and talent shows. Others felt that this short pier on its untidy angled piles spoiled the long continuous sweep of the bay. The bandstand lasted forty-seven years and was becoming dilapidated when the decision was made to remove the pier section in 1986. The building on the Esplanade was retained and, extensively refurbished, is now an attractive feature on the sea front.*

# Bury Street

*Bury Street, 1975*

In 1975 a once picturesque row of five cottages was awaiting demolition and three of the houses stand empty and boarded up. Close to the town centre, off St Nicholas Street, this was Bury Street, taking its name from a little cemetery at the end of the street. Clearance of these cottages and an adjacent warehouse in Bury Street, the graveyard and a chapel in Lower Bond Street provided the site for Weymouth's first multi-storey car park and superstore and thus all trace of Bury Street was removed from the local map.

*Bury Street, 2003*

The site of the little mansard-roofed cottages in Bury Street is now lost beneath the latest developments off St Nicholas Street. Plans for the reconstruction of a large area of Lower Bond Street and Commercial Road were to fall through several times before the eventual completion of the 'New Bond Street' shopping centre in 2000. The supermarket which replaced the cottages (later used as an indoor market prior to its demolition) has been replaced in turn by a multiplex cinema.

*The remains of those buried in the Bury Street graveyard were reinterred at Westham in the 1970s and this particularly interesting headstone was put on display in Weymouth Museum. It records the death in 1832 of Lieutenant Thomas Knight, chief officer of the Lulworth Coast Guard, who was beaten senseless and thrown over a cliff as he attempted to arrest a gang of local smugglers. It was a funeral of great pomp and ceremony, and walking in the procession were Lieutenant Knight's widow and five children.*

*Lost now under late-twentieth-century development, the little graveyard which gave Bury Street its name was behind the Methodist chapel in Lower Bond Street and once provided a peaceful patch of green in the town centre. It was used for town burials when there was no longer any space left in St Mary's churchyard and before the large cemeteries opened at Westham in the 1850s.*

*Seen here shortly before demolition in the 1970s, Webb Major's store in Lower Bond Street was formerly the Wesleyan Methodist Chapel. Built in 1805, the chapel closed in 1867 when Maiden Street Methodist Church was completed.*

# Christchurch, King Street

*Christchurch, c.1900*

This imposing church in King Street would have provided their first glimpse of Weymouth for many thousands of holidaymakers streaming out of the railway station, as it stood almost opposite the station entrance from 1874 until 1956. The view is taken from Queen Street. Christchurch, designed by Ewan Christian, was a chapel of ease to St Mary's Church and it was built to serve the growing population at the northern end of the town when the 'Park District' land was developed as housing in the latter half of the nineteenth century. By the 1930s the church's congregations had declined and it closed. After war service as a club for evacuees and a British Restaurant, no permanent use could be found for Christchurch and it was demolished. Traces of the old church still remain in the borough, as some of its stone was used in houses then being built at the top end of Radipole Lake, and interior fittings were transferred to St Aldhelm's Church in Spa Road, Radipole. On the opposite corner of King Street/Park Street the original Queen's Hotel can be seen. This pub was completely rebuilt in the 1930s and was intended to herald the proposed new and much extended Weymouth railway station which never materialised; war and the decline of the rail network ended any planned expansion and only in 1986 was Weymouth Station rebuilt, and then on a much reduced scale.

*Christchurch, 2003*

In 2003 the scene is greatly changed. The only architectural feature from the old photograph is the tall building on the left, belonging then to the Victorian Eye Infirmary and now to the British Legion. Christchurch has been replaced by the flats and shops of Garnet Court and the Queen's Hotel is a red-brick rebuild of the old pub on the same site. The King Street/Queen Street junction is one of Weymouth's traffic 'hotspots' and the street scene is cluttered with road markings, traffic lights, signs and crossings. The 'Queen's' probably takes its name from the street almost opposite. Several pubs close to this road junction have closed (the Ranelagh, at the end of Ranelagh Road, and the Fountain, the Half Moon and the Portland Railway Hotel in King Street), or have been renamed (the Clifton and the Terminus in Queen Street are now the Railway Station and the Giant Pot respectively). The name of the Somerset Hotel remains unchanged and the Sun in King Street has reverted to its original title after being known as King's in recent years.

*A delightful Edwardian scene at the entrance to Weymouth railway station. The station was a Brunel-designed building dating back to 1857 when the railway to Weymouth opened. The photograph is taken from the Wood family's album of holiday snapshots, which is now in Weymouth Library's Local Studies Collection. Alfred Wood, his wife and children regularly spent their summer holidays in Weymouth in the early years of the twentieth century.*

*The original station was in a very dilapidated state when it was eventually replaced in 1986 by this rather featureless railway terminus fronted by a vast expanse of tarmac, its outlook softened slightly by a small sculpture garden in the centre.*

# Colwell House, School Street

*Colwell House, c.1950*

The Weymouth Royal Hospital and Dispensary in School Street is probably best remembered by long-time Weymouth residents as the Salvation Army Hostel, providing the homeless with food and accommodation for more than fifty years. The Salvation Army took over the building when the hospital closed on its amalgamation in the 1920s with Weymouth and District Hospital in Melcombe Avenue. The Royal

Hospital (it was under the patronage of Princess Charlotte, grand-daughter of King George III, and her husband Prince Leopold) had been founded in the town in 1816 'for the relief of the sick poor, with advice, medicine and attendance, and for the cowpock inoculation, preventing the extension and fatality of infectious diseases and keeping multitudes of the sick poor from the necessity of throwing themselves into parochial workhouses'. The site for the building was purchased in 1867 and the hospital opened on 18 May 1872, later extending into the adjacent property. In 1981 the Salvation Army Hostel, known as Colwell House, was forced to close owing to lack of sufficient funds to do repairs.

*Colwell House, 2003*

In 1983 the old Royal Hospital building was demolished and its site was redeveloped as an indoor shopping centre, taking its name – the 'Colwell Centre' – from the surname of one of Weymouth's twentieth century Salvationists. A link with the hospital has also been preserved; mounted on the outside wall of the Colwell Centre is a plaque once on the old building which provides a little of the history of this early-nineteenth-century philanthropic institution.

*Salvation Army services were held in various premises in the town until the purpose-built Citadel was erected on the corner of Westham Road and Park Street in 1903.*

# Commercial Road

*Commercial Road, 1965*

The 1965 scene shows Commercial Road at its junction with Westham Road as the Channel Islands boat train slowly makes its way to Weymouth railway station before embarking on its journey to London Waterloo behind a mainline loco (until 1959 the London terminus for the service had been Paddington).  It is preceded by the all-important flagman with his red flag ensuring that it is safe for the train to proceed.  Presumably at this point the train is stationary since the lady in the centre of the photograph is crossing the road directly in front of the engine's 'Danger. Keep 50 feet clear' warning board!  The Weymouth Harbour Tramway opened in 1865 providing a much needed link between the Great Western Railway Company's cargo and passenger steamers at the pier and Weymouth railway station.  Trains were initially horse-drawn until steam was introduced on the line in the 1880s, giving way to diesel locos in the early 1960s.  The rolling stock for the mainline trains trundling through Weymouth's street was an everyday feature of local life, its slow progress often further impeded by carelessly parked cars obstructing the line. Electrification of the Weymouth–Waterloo line in 1988 brought the tramway service to a close.  The New Bridge Inn is shown on the left of the picture, Melcombe Regis School on the right, and in the centre stands Bethany Hall.

*Commercial Road, 2003*

In 2003 the Harbour Tramway's railway lines and Bethany Hall are the only recognisable features from the earlier photograph.  Today only the very occasional 'special' uses the tramway's lines and although commercial interests have experimented with a tram service along the route, no definite plans have yet materialised.  The rubble-strewn site on the left bears witness to the recent demise of the New Bridge Inn, demolished in February 2003.  The Gospel Hall opened in 1888 and its side wall still bears a plaque inscribed 'George Street Hall', a reminder of the days when Westham Road was known as 'Little George Street'.  The large building beyond is Debenham's department store – part of the 1990s town-centre redevelopment.  The latest occupant of the site beside Westham Bridge, formerly occupied by Melcombe Regis School, is Weymouth Marina, which overlooks the once empty and dreary Inner Harbour, now much improved and filled with pleasure craft.  The school had provided primary education for the town's children from 1911 until its closure in 1970, and from 1972 the building housed Weymouth Museum until 1989, when the museum's collections relocated to Brewer's Quay, in Hope Square.

*A 1950s reminder of the age of steam on the Weymouth Harbour Tramway.  This is GWR Pannier Tank 1367 on Custom House Quay, the shunting locomotive having stopped outside Allways Haulage and Removals building (in 2003 the offices of the Weymouth Harbourmaster).  No. 1367 was the first standard Great Western engine to come into service on the Tramway, arriving in 1935 and staying until 1962.  Behind the loco can be seen a freight lorry – one of many which eventually saw the ending of the bulk of railway goods traffic throughout the British Isles.*

*The outward appearance of Melcombe Regis School changed little after its conversion to Weymouth's first museum in 1972.  The museum was a development of the very successful 'Quatercentenary' Local History Exhibition staged here in 1971 to commemorate the 400th anniversary of the union of the two formerly separate boroughs of Weymouth and Melcombe Regis into one town in 1571.*

# Cosens' Cold Store, West Street

*Cosens' Cold Store, 1968*

This building, with its entrance at the end of West Street, was owned throughout most of the twentieth century by local marine engineers Cosens & Company. It was at the rear of their works in Commercial Road and in the 1920s the company converted it from former use as a foundry to become Cosens' Cold Store, installing an ice-making plant and storing meat and other perishables (Sansinena's – the firm whose name appears above the entrance – were major meat wholesalers). The photograph dates from 1968 and was taken a few months before the ice store was demolished, modern commercial and domestic refrigeration techniques having brought about a marked decline in its use. Prior to Cosens' ownership, the building had an interesting history. Dating from 1804, it was originally built as a Congregational Chapel and the entrance was in West Street. Its use as a place of worship ceased when Gloucester Street Congregational Church was completed in 1864. The windows, although bricked up in this 1968 view, provide some indication of its previous history. In the 1880s the former chapel was converted to become the Theatre Royal, the second theatre in Weymouth to bear this name, the first having been located on the sea front in Georgian times. A long entrance passageway led into the building from St Nicholas Street, but its theatrical life was short, competition from the nearby Jubilee Hall, purpose built and opened in the late 1880s, proving to be too great. Its next use was as a foundry, casting items as diverse as ships' propellers and iron tombstones – and some of the latter can still be seen today in local cemeteries. How many buildings can claim in their lifetime to have been a chapel, theatre, foundry, cold store and, finally and ignominiously, a car park?

*Cosens' Cold Store, 2003*

In 2003 much of old West Street has been demolished and rebuilt, with period-style cottages replacing the former terraces which had included the Butcher's Arms public house. The old chapel which had been converted as a cold store was demolished in 1968 and its site became part of a car park off St Nicholas Street. Now the chapel site is lost in the car-parking area adjacent to the Lakeside Superbowl where it is overlooked by these tall harbourside apartment blocks, which in the 1990s replaced the former industries of West Street and Commercial Road.

THEATRE ROYAL, WEYMOUTH.

*The 1804 Congregational Chapel, seen from West Street, is recreated here in a drawing by the late Eric Ricketts; the tall windows are very recognisable in the 1968 photograph opposite.*

*This Victorian engraving illustrates the entrance in St Nicholas Street used by theatre patrons as they walked down the long corridor to the actual Theatre Royal, visible in the background. Following demolition of the chapel/theatre/foundry/coldstore in 1968, this entrance arch was preserved for a few years, but it too was removed from St Nicholas Street in the 1980s.*

# Cox's Foundry, Ranelagh Road

*Cox's Foundry, c.1900*

The foundry building of R. Cox & Son stood at the end of Ranelagh Road. The business was originally established in 1839 at Quebec Place off Park Street and Cox would have moved here towards the end of the nineteenth century as the Park District developed. The works were originally known as the Park Foundry, renamed the Paragon Foundry when the next proprietor took them over in the late 1920s. Many Weymouth residents will remember the foundry as the Vixen Forge, well known for the decorative wrought-ironwork which was produced here in the 1950s and early 1960s. By the mid-1960s an engineering works had taken over on the site.

*Cox's Foundry, 2003*

In 2003 all trace of the old foundry has gone and the apartments of Heron Court fill the site. The end house (No 55) of the adjacent Victorian terrace, which stood close to the foundry, has also been demolished, but its neighbour – just seen on the extreme right of the old photograph – still stands.

*Just north of Heron Court, Alexander Bridge crosses the railway lines at the end of Cassiobury Road, linking this old part of the town to Radipole Park Gardens (now renamed Princess Diana Gardens) and Radipole Park Drive. The bridge was the gift of William Henry Alexander, a wealthy lawyer and generous benefactor of many worthy causes, local and national. In Weymouth he made generous donations to the Princess Christian Hospital (later Weymouth and District Hospital) when it was built in the early 1900s, but he is perhaps best known for his offer to pay for the cost of a building in London to house the National Portrait Gallery. A condition of the donation was that he should select the architect of the project – his choice being Ewan Christian, an eminent ecclesiastical architect who was also the architect of Christchurch in Weymouth. W.H. Alexander died in 1905 and is buried in Radipole churchyard. Plans are afoot to replace the bridge with one which will give easier access from the Radipole Park Drive side.*

*Standing on the corner of Brownlow Street, the Brownlow Hotel is the only public house still remaining in Ranelagh Road. The land on which the Park District houses stand was purchased in the latter half of the nineteenth century by the Conservative Land Agency and the streets built on it were named after contemporary Tory politicians. The 3rd Earl Brownlow served in Lord Salisbury's government in the 1880s.*

# Custom House Quay

*Custom House Quay, 1950s*

The quay in the 1950s viewed from Trinity Road across the harbour with, tied up alongside, the Royal Air Force Vessel *Airmoor II*. She was one of a number of RAF support craft, all conversions from different roles, which made use of the harbour facilities whilst in the local area attending upon the practice bombing targets positioned in West Bay (Lyme Bay) as part of the Royal Air Force Chesil Bank Bombing Ranges facility. They were used to tow the targets (wooden, painted yellow – and later 'dayglo' red – and with pole and basket identifiers) either to Ferrybridge or to Weymouth itself for routine maintenance before repositioning them back off the Chesil. The harbourside buildings behind the *Airmoor II* can still be seen today, although changes of occupancy have taken place. On the left was the tall warehouse of John Deheer, mainly used for the storage of imported fertiliser products until a dip in trade in the 1960s caused its closure. Next to it was the head office of long-established marine engineers Cosens & Co., owners of the local paddle-steamer fleet. The decline in popularity of steamer excursions led to Cosens selling this building in 1962 and concentrating activities at their works in Commercial Road. The chapel in the centre of the picture was founded in 1866 as a Sailors' Bethel and stands on the quayside site occupied in Georgian times by Hot and Cold Seawater Baths, where visitors nervous of immersing themselves in the bay could enjoy the benefits of a 'dip' on dry land. The Bethel provided a place of worship and a reading room for seamen until 1950. Allways' big furniture depository and warehouse stood next to one of the few private dwellings on the quayside, a bow-windowed house on the corner of South Parade.

### Custom House Quay, 2003

In 2003 Deheer's warehouse is occupied by a maritime-themed tourist attraction, the 'Deep Sea Adventure', an appropriate use for this massive building which has overlooked the harbourside since the mid-nineteenth century. Cosens' former offices currently house a small indoor market and the Victorian Sailors' Bethel has become HQ of the Royal Dorset Yacht Club, following its use as a popular restaurant – 'The Spinnaker' – and prior to that as the meeting place of Weymouth Youth Club. The Weymouth Harbourmaster's office is now in the Allways building.

*One of the most important buildings on Custom House Quay, and probably originally built for one of the town's wealthiest merchants, the former Custom House dates from the early nineteenth century. Above its doorway are the Royal Arms, finely detailed in cast iron. The building also has RAF connections, for it was used as the headquarters building of No 40 RAF Air Sea Rescue and Marine Craft Unit, which was based at Weymouth from April 1944 until June 1946 and had a commendable war record to look back upon on disbandment. Today it is occupied by the very busy Portland Coastguard, whose area of responsibility stretches from the Dorset/Hampshire border at Chewton Bunny in the east, to Exmouth in the west and out to mid-Channel.*

*The Royal Air Forces Association Club in Maiden Street occupies part of Weymouth's earliest group of historic buildings. From the harbourside Ship Inn on Custom House Quay to the Duke of Cornwall public house on the corner of St Edmund Street these all date from the seventeenth century. The Royal Air Force's last operational connection with the local area was the employment of RAF air traffic controllers on exchange duty at the Portland helicopter base, but this ceased in March 1999 when the air station closed down as a military facility. Nevertheless, the RAFA continues to thrive in the borough, its club room in Maiden Street being a mere stone's throw away from where the junior service's high-speed launches were once moored, awaiting their next scramble call.*

# D-Day Memories

*D-Day Memories, 1944*

Weymouth and Portland were two of the major embarkation ports for the vast Allied invasion force which crossed the Channel and landed on the Normandy beaches at dawn on D-Day, 6 June 1944. Code-named *Operation Overlord* this was to be the biggest amphibious invasion in history and 517,816 troops and 144,093 vehicles were to leave Weymouth and Portland harbours between D-Day and the end of the war. Here, American soldiers and British sailors carry out pre-invasion exercises aboard LCAs (Landing Craft, Assault) in the weeks prior to the D-Day. Across the harbour on Nothe Parade can be seen the slipways and workshops of local marine engineers Cosens & Co. They were to be kept busy throughout the war years, maintaining and repairing a steady stream of vessels on government service. Cosens ceased using this site early in the 1960s and their building has been demolished. The land on which it stood is now a boatyard for Weymouth Sailing Club, current occupants of the flat-roofed building on the right.

*D-Day Memories, 2003*

Nearly sixty years after D-Day the former Coastguard cottages in Barrack Road still overlook the harbour, but the vessels we see are those of peace and not hostilities – many being stored ashore here for the winter months, but soon to give pleasure to their crews in the beautiful waters of Weymouth Bay and further afield. Today, to the left of the rebuilt Cosens slipway building, behind which can be seen the stone steps leading up to the Nothe, the Weymouth RNLI's inshore-rescue boat is stored and launched.

*The American Memorial commemorates the part played by US forces in the Allied victory and bears a plaque presented to the town by the 14th Major Port, US Army. As D-Day ended, more than 3000 American servicemen who had left here to carry out the initial assault on Omaha Beach and Pointe du Hoc were dead, wounded or unaccounted for. The memorial was unveiled on 3 December 1947 by Major General Clayton L Bissell, DSC, DFC, the US Military and Air Attaché. There is a further memorial in the Victoria Gardens, Portland.*

*The MV* My Girl, *the furthest from the camera of the three vessels seen here tied up in the Inner Harbour outside the Municipal Offices, played her own essential part in the war effort, both before and after D-Day. Built in 1931, she was commandeered on the outbreak of hostilities in 1939, and spent the war years under the control of the naval authorities. Skippered by her owner Ron Hill, she ferried men and matériel to and from the Royal Artillery-manned defensive installations on the breakwater arms surrounding Portland Harbour, sailing over 20,000 nautical miles and carrying over 250,000 troops in military service. Back in service as a pleasure craft, she still sails her wartime haunts off Portland, proudly flying the pennant of the Royal Artillery and with a commemorative plaque recording her service to the nation mounted in the cabin.*

*In recent years new annotations commemorate the losses of United States personnel in* Exercise Tiger *in April 1944 and aboard the troopship* Leopoldville *on Christmas Day of the same year. The memorial, the light atop which is never switched off, is a focal point for the many US war veterans who return to the local area to remember fallen colleagues and meet with surviving comrades-in-arms from more than half a century ago. Every year on Remembrance Sunday a short service is held here after the main service at the town's war memorial adjacent to the Pier Bandstand.*

# Echo Office, St Thomas Street

*Echo Office, 1950*

The local daily paper is the *Dorset Echo*, published late morning, Monday through to Saturday. It started in 1921 as the *Dorset Daily Echo* and became the *Dorset Evening Echo* in 1958, changing its name to *Dorset Echo* on Thursday 11 March 1999. Prior to 1921 locals obtained most of their news from the weekly *Southern Times*, which was published in Weymouth from the early 1850s until 1964. The *Echo's* printing works and offices occupied this site in St Thomas Street, which extended through to St Nicholas Street, but this is a post-Second-World-War building. In one of the town's worst air raids on 2 April 1942, the *Echo* works were so seriously damaged that printing had to be transferred to the company's Bournemouth offices for the rest of the war and until the Weymouth premises could be rebuilt. The picture dates from the 1950s when the poster in the office window promised 'All the News for 2d'.

*Some fifty years after the postwar rebuild of the town premises, the new out-of-town offices and printing works of the* Dorset Echo, *on the Granby Industrial Estate at Chickerell reflect a major change in architectural style.*

*Echo Office, 2003*

The *Echo* moved out of the town centre in 1999, although an office in St Mary Street is maintained. The paper is now printed at the company's new headquarters in Hampshire Road on the Granby Industrial Estate, with the St Thomas Street building having been converted to a wine bar and eatery owned by the Yates chain.

*Opposite the* Echo *offices in St Thomas Street stood the old Swan Inn. The building appears to have been used as a small brewery in the nineteenth century, which was later taken over by the Hope Square brewer John Groves, who turned the premises into a pub. It and the neighbouring properties to the south – Darch's shop selling furniture, radios, cycles, mopeds and scooters, and the Town Bridge Café, were demolished in 1975 and the block was rebuilt, occupied firstly by Centre News and later, by newsagent and bookseller John Menzies. Now it is once again back in business as a pub and eating place, with the current owners Wetherspoon having restored its original name 'The Swan'.*

# Fleet Review, 1938

*Fleet Review, 1938*

A spectacular photograph from July 1938 as the Home Fleet assembles in Weymouth Bay awaiting a visit from King George VI. The King, accompanied by the Duke of Kent, arrived in the Royal Train and was driven through cheering crowds to the pier where he embarked on the royal barge for the short trip to the Royal Yacht *Victoria and Albert*. Transferring to the flagship HMS *Nelson*, the King later accompanied the fleet of some 60 ships to sea and watched exercises in the Channel. The Second World War was less than a year away and in the fleet was the aircraft carrier HMS *Courageous* which was to be sunk by U-29 off the Hebrides on 17 September 1939, just two weeks after the outbreak of hostilities.

*Fleet Review, 2003*

The bay itself was empty of all vessels when we visited Bowleaze Coveway to take the modern photograph, but three RN warships were exercising on the southern horizon, bringing back memories of 'The Thursday Wars' which took place when NATO ships worked up locally. The Isle of Portland stands proud beyond the breakwater arms. With the exception of the helicopter base, the Royal Navy left Portland on 21 July 1995, when Flag Officer Sea Training departed onboard HMS *Argyll* for Devonport.

*In June 1938 before embarking in the Royal Barge, King George VI inspected a Royal Marine guard of honour assembled on the pier in front of the old Pavilion Theatre.*

*Just over a year later, on 21 July 1939, the King was back in Weymouth, on an unofficial visit prior to embarking in the Royal Yacht for a journey to Dartmouth. He was accompanied by Queen Elizabeth, and the young Princesses Elizabeth and Margaret who were presented with bouquets by local schoolgirls Josephine Dowle and Vivien Atkins. On 9 August, with the outbreak of the Second World War less than four weeks away, the King returned to Weymouth once more, this time to review the Reserve Fleet, after which the ships prepared to sail to their battle stations.*

# Forte's Corner

*Forte's Corner, c.1905*

The first Great Western Railway buses appeared in Weymouth in 1905 and this photograph probably dates from around that period. Milnes-Daimler LC 1172 stands outside Royal Terrace prior to departing for Radipole. The house in the centre of the picture, with foliage in its ground-floor window boxes, no longer exists. This was No. 18 Royal

Terrace and it was demolished in 1929 to allow for road widening at this narrow and busy entrance to Westham Road. The terrace on the left is Frederick Place, where the most striking alteration later in the twentieth century would be the conversion of No. 1, on the corner of Westham Road, to Forte's Ice Cream Parlor and Restaurant.

*Forte's Corner, 2003*

The scene in 2003 shows that No. 17 Royal Terrace (on the extreme right of the previous photograph) has become the building on the corner of Westham Road, following No. 18's demolition, and that the road is considerably wider. No. 1 Frederick Place, once Forte's, is now the Hogshead pub and at ground level a few shop fronts have appeared in place of the original bow windows shown in the earlier picture.

*Frederick Place was built in the 1830s and No. 1, shown here in 1909, appears to be of a slightly different design from the rest of the terrace. Its entrance is at the side of the building and where one would expect to find the front door is a bricked-in 'blind' window. If this was an alteration it must have been made quite early in the terrace's history as the side entrance is shown on large-scale town maps of the 1860s.*

*The arrival in the town in the early 1930s of the Forte family brought about great changes to No. 1 Frederick Place, with plate glass at street level, additional windows in the storeys above and an extension in Westham Road. Nevertheless, the building – seen here in the 1950s – is still very recognisable today. The Fortes, all of whom came from a small village in Italy, went on to own many of the UK's major hotels and restaurants. On Weymouth sea front a second Forte's café opened in Brunswick Terrace in the 1930s (now Hamiltons).*

# Franchise Street

*Franchise Street, c.1905*

This view of Franchise Street dates from the early 1900s and shows a long terrace of houses which was badly damaged during the Second World War and totally cleared after the war ended. Just visible at the end of the street is the Chapelhay Tavern and on the extreme right-hand side of the picture is a glimpse of a little shop which is still there today. Chapelhay suffered repeated Second World War air attacks and on 17 November 1940 a parachute mine landed between Chapelhay Street and Franchise Street, killing several people and causing many injuries and tremendous damage, mostly suffered by those who lived in this terrace.

*Franchise Street, 2003*

Postwar rebuilding of Chapelhay in the 1950s included Chapelhay Heights, council flats to replace the old blitzed terraces, plus a shopping precinct and new pub – the Prospect. This view of 2003 shows the flats which replaced the bombed terrace, and the shop (right) which appears on both pictures. Pre-war Chapelhay does not seem to have been much photographed. It was an ordinary town area of terraced houses and shops, not worthy of a picture-postcard view, yet very much a real community. Many of Chapelhay's old street and terrace names disappeared in the twentieth century – Quebec Place, Southampton Row, Ebenezer Place, Salem Place, Newton Place, Queen's Row, East Row and West Row have all gone. Gordon Row, taking its name from the bombed General Gordon pub, has been retained in the postwar street of new shops.

*Another victim of the 1940 air raids on Chapelhay was Holy Trinity School, hit more than once but most severely damaged on 17 November, after which it could not be used again as a school. This has been an unfortunate site in time of war. In the seventeenth century the chapel of St Nicholas (the 'chapel' which gave Chapelhay, or, the Chapelry its name) stood here and was converted for use as a fort in the bitter local fighting of the English Civil War, during which it was so badly damaged that it was never again used as a place of worship. Holy Trinity School, designed by Talbot Bury, built by Weymouth builder Philip Dodson in 1853 and opened in 1854, was demolished in 1961 (the children of the parish moved in 1952 to new school buildings in Cross Road, having been educated in temporary classrooms in buildings around the town following the bombing). Housing – Trinity Court – now stands here at the top of Chapelhay Steps, which lead conveniently down to the harbour and town centre.*

*The remains of the terrace (opposite, top) after the mine explosion of 17 November 1940. With the war in Europe over in 1945, Weymouth began to return to normality, but there was no short-term way to renovate the extensive damage to parts of the town and local traders made the best of what was available to them. With buddleia – the archetypal bomb-site shrub – already beginning to run wild at Chaplehay, two shops soon reopened for business at patched-up ground-floor level: Skillman the electricians and a general store and green-grocer's, which were just beyond these bombed buildings. Chaplehay was the most heavily bombed part of the resort, and would almost certainly have been on the receiving end of Axis bombs and landmines in error, for the true target would have been the harbour lying tucked below the heights.*

# George Inn, Custom House Quay

*George Inn, c.1870*

This photograph of the George Inn on Weymouth quayside was taken around 1870. The ancient building, dating back to Tudor or Stuart times was once owned by Sir Samuel Mico, a wealthy and influential London merchant and ship owner with a range of commercial and shipping interests in Weymouth. Mico, who was knighted in 1645 and died in 1660, was one of the most powerful businessmen of his day. In his will, he remembered his links with Weymouth by making a number of charitable bequests. Included in these was the gift to Melcombe Regis of 'his house standing at the east end of the quay of that town called the George Tavern or Inn, with the yards and any other ground thereto belonging, with the profits thereof, to put out three poor children apprentices yearly'. In Mico's day there was little development seaward along what is now Custom House Quay and the George occupied a prominent position at the entrance to Weymouth Harbour.

*George Inn, 2003*

The original George Inn was demolished in the 1880s to make way for the present, larger hostelry of the same name (the three-storey building on the right) – which has a plaque on its external wall telling of its links with Samuel Mico, whose Trust continues to this day. In 2003 it funded nine young people to become apprentice engineers and still makes grants to retired mariners. Buildings at the lower end of Maiden Street appear in both pictures – the Fish Market of 1855 with its extended roofline, and beyond it much older stone buildings of the seventeenth century. The big warehouse on the left-hand side of the old photograph was demolished in 1958 and two-storey extensions to the Ship Inn now fill the site.

*Today's George Inn sign is fittingly based on a famous portrait of King George III, who brought Weymouth fame as royalty's favourite health and pleasure resort, but the name of the original inn predates all the Georges who have been crowned kings of Great Britain and Ireland. 'The George' is one of the country's most popular pub names and probably derives from St George, the patron saint of England.*

*In 1855 two new market houses opened in Weymouth. The larger building, in St Mary Street, accommodated a selection of indoor shops and stalls, but it was demolished in 1939, whilst the second market, seen here, was designed exclusively for the sale of fish. It was not a success initially, being so close to the busy harbour with dusty cargoes being loaded and unloaded and smoke from the steamer funnels depositing sooty smuts on the fish for sale. Eventually the little market became a store for bulk fertilisers, which had to be removed in some haste in 1962 when the building's Maiden Street wall began to bulge ominously. It was repaired, and in today's much cleaner harbourside air the Victorian Fish Market has happily reverted to its original purpose of selling fresh fish and the locally famous crabs.*

# Gloucester Lodge

*Gloucester Lodge, c.1923*

Gloucester Lodge was built in 1780 by William Frederick, Duke of Gloucester, the younger brother of King George III. The Duke was a frequent visitor to Southampton and the New Forest, from where he made excursions to Weymouth in the 1760s and 1770s, finding the place and the company to his liking. His 'Lodge', quite modest by royal standards, is the central building with the lower roofline in this photograph from the early 1920s. The large extension on the left-hand side is a Victorian addition and in Georgian times long gardens, known as 'The Shrubbery' swept right down into the town from the Lodge. Here, after his illness of 1788, King George III came to recuperate and test the efficacy of sea bathing, highly recommended as a cure-all by the physicians of the day. His brother's house proved to be on the small side for the royal entourage and some of King George's servants had to be boarded out around the town, rising early to dash through the streets and carry out their duties at the Lodge. Weymouth suited the King very well and he spent 14 holidays in the resort between 1789 and 1805. In 1820 Gloucester Lodge was sold and a little later in the nineteenth century it became the Gloucester Hotel, to which the extension was added. Prior to this the entrance had been at the side of the building, through the gardens, but the hotel's new front entrance led directly on to the Esplanade.

*Gloucester Lodge, 2003*

Rather altered today, the building has had an extra storey added, plus a double row of attics in the roof, bringing it to the same height as the adjacent extension. The rebuilding was the result of a disastrous fire in March 1927, when the interior of the Gloucester Hotel was almost completely burnt out. The façade of the old building was saved and it is quite possible that King George III once stood at one of the Venetian windows on the ground floor contemplating the waters of the bay in which he was soon to be 'dipped'. The hotel was converted to residential and office use in the 1980s and has now reverted to its original name Gloucester Lodge.

*Gloucester Lodge was not the first of the buildings to face the sea at Weymouth as the town began to turn its attention away from the harbour, its former main source of income. Doctors promoting the seaside health cure had brought visitors to Weymouth from the middle of the eighteenth century and in the 1770s this bow-fronted purpose-built hotel appeared on the sea front. Many other Esplanade buildings would follow once the royal visits got under way. Originally known as Stacy's Hotel, the proprietors renamed it the Royal Hotel when their royal neighbours began frequenting the hotel's fashionable Assembly Rooms. Note the little stones, once linked by chains, which define the Esplanade – very few of these remain today, many having been uprooted in a great storm which destroyed much of the promenade in 1824.*

*The old Royal Hotel proved too small and too restrained in its design for the Victorians, who demolished it in 1891, replacing it a few years later with the present ornate Royal Hotel which, despite its flamboyant style, does not look out of place among the plainer neighbouring terraces. Unlike the former Gloucester Hotel, the Royal continues today as one of the resort's major hotels.*

*A few of the stones, such as this one with a small plaque telling its history, have been preserved and can still be found on the Esplanade opposite the Pier Bandstand. A further stone built into one of the raised flower beds towards the southern end of the promenade is inscribed with the details of the 1824 Great Gale.*

# Gloucester Street Congregational Church

*Gloucester Street Congregational Church, c.1870*

Gloucester Street Congregational Church opened on 22 July 1864, the congregation formerly having worshipped at the West Street Chapel, with new church's first minister being the Reverend R.S. Ashton. As seen in this 1870 view, the twin-spired building on the corner of Park Street and Gloucester Street overlooked an inlet of Radipole Lake, then used as a timber-curing pond. The terrace on the left and the house on the right still exist, although the church and timber pond have gone. It is difficult to believe, standing here today, that so much land has been reclaimed from the Lake in the 20th Century and that Commercial Road was in fact a harbour wall along here until extensive infilling took place in the 1920s, providing land for Melcombe Regis Gardens and Radipole Park Drive.

*Gloucester Street Congregational Church, 2003*

Viewed some 130 years later, the Congregational Church has gone. The imposing church, built on insecure foundations, was demolished in 1980, its congregation having joined with worshippers at the United Reformed Church in Hope Square. The apartments which replaced it are named George Thorne House, after one of the town's early Nonconformist ministers. For many years the huge timber sheds of Betts (later Webb Major's) timber yard stood on the infilled timber pond but these too disappeared in the early 1980s and yet another open space has been given over to car parking (now Park Street car park).

*Scenes from the wedding on 20 February 1965 of Mr Paul Schmid and Miss Jennifer Dicks show the impressive organ which once graced the church and the ornate pillars abutting the entrance steps. The bride's father, Mr Harry Dicks (seen to the right of the wedding party on the steps), was a well-known Weymouth character, once a jeweller and clock maker, later an antique dealer and always a contented artist and extrovert!*

# Greenhill Gardens

*Greenhill Gardens, c.1880*

Greenhill Gardens, at the northern end of the Esplanade, were laid out
on land given to the town in the 1870s by Sir Frederic Johnstone, a
generous gift – but Sir Frederic owned vast amounts of land in Weymouth
for which he collected enormous sums in ground rents. The view shows
the gardens in their early years, laid out mainly with lawns and shrubs.
The spire of St John's Church dominates the skyline in the middle

distance, with the magnificent sweep of Weymouth Bay, before the building of the Pier Bandstand, uncluttered by beach huts or the other paraphernalia of the seaside in summer.

*Greenhill Gardens, 2003*

In 2003 the gardens are much more attractively landscaped with path-ways surrounded by flower-beds and summer plants specially chosen for their fragrance and labelled in Braille to enhance their enjoyment by the visually impaired. A putting green, from which our photograph was taken, tennis courts and a 'county standard' bowling green are all later additions to the original gardens.

*The Greenhill Gardens' Floral Clock, installed by James Ritchie of Edinburgh in 1936, was a summer attraction for decades until the clock hands became too much of a regular target for vandals. Nearby in the gardens, one large semi-circular flower-bed is themed each summer to celebrate a special event or anniversary.*

*The weather vane in the gardens was officially unveiled on Friday 30 May 1952, with the text on the plinth below the stone column reading: 'This weathervane commemorates the establishment of a world speed record of 406.92 mph on 29 September 1931 by Flight Lieutenant G.H. Stainforth AFC, an old boy of Weymouth College and a member of the Schneider Trophy Team. The aircraft of which this is a replica was the prototype [sic] of the Battle of Britain Spitfire. Originally erected over the college in July 1932, the vane was presented to the borough when the college closed in 1940 and was mounted in its present position in May 1952.'*

*George Stainforth, by then a wing commander and flying Beaufighters as OC No 89 Squadron, was killed in North Africa on 27 September 1942 and lies buried at the Commonwealth War Graves Commission Cemetery at Ismâilîa in Egypt. Deteriorating from continuous exposure to the local salt air, the vane was taken down and refurbished in the late 1960s by local classic car enthusiast Jim Avery.*

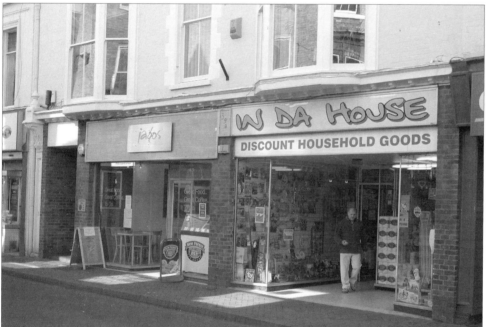

# Hawkes, Freeman & Co, St Thomas Street

*Hawkes, Freeman & Co, c.1910*

There were obviously few restrictions on the use of pavement and roadway as display space when this photograph of the Hawkes, Freeman shop, at No. 39 St Thomas Street, was taken in the early years of the twentieth century. The firm, founded in 1845, described itself as house furnishers, carpet importers and factors, cabinet manufacturers, carpenters and joiners, upholsterers, decorators, removal contractors, warehousemen, house and estate agents and valuers, and funeral furnishers ... and this was only at the store above – it provided another list of its services at a second store, then on the Town Bridge. The firm acquired an adjacent site south of the building shown for a large new shop in the late 1930s.

*Hawkes, Freeman & Co, 2003*

The carved column on the extreme left-hand side of the old picture can still be seen, with the windows above being equally recognisable today; however, shop alterations have seen the removal of the major part of the right-hand column. Now two separate shops, the one on the right does have a tenuous link with Hawkes, Freeman in that it offers for sale some not dissimilar articles of household wares.

*When Hawkes, Freeman moved south from No. 39 St Thomas Street, their new shop was built partly on the site of the former Bear Inn. The Bear's front entrance, shown here, was in St Mary Street, with its yard and stables extending through to St Thomas Street. The old hostelry had ceased trading in 1929.*

*Today the trend is for shop selling goods such as those vended by Hawkes, Freeman to be located on out-of-town sites, and Weymouth is no exception. Here we see the B&Q store in Jubilee Close – site of the former railway coach and truck sidings – selling what we now know as DIY and house makeover products, but which the Victorians would have known as ironmongery.*

# Hope Square

*Hope Square, 1920s*

A wonderful 1920s scene in Hope Square, as staff from John Groves Brewery prepare for the firm's annual outing with their families, space no doubt being found on the already laden charabancs for a good few bottles of their employer's famous ales! The brewery building dates from 1904, and stood next to the much older Devenish Brewery – the rival firms eventually amalgamating in 1960. The vehicles are the local Rambler company's fleet.

*Hope Square, 2003*

The brewing industry ceased operations in Weymouth in 1984 and five years later the former John Groves brewery and adjacent buildings were converted to become Brewer's Quay, a tourist attraction housing 'The Timewalk', a special-effects journey through Weymouth's history; Weymouth Museum (which relocated here from the old Melcombe Regis School at Westham Bridge); a shopping village; cafés and a pub. Hope Square is now a place to linger, with outdoor seating, trees and flowers combining with harbour views to make this one of the resort's most attractive areas. Virtually all of the other brewing sites in the town have also been converted to new uses – mainly to housing, and include the aptly named The Maltings and Barley Way, off Rodwell Avenue.

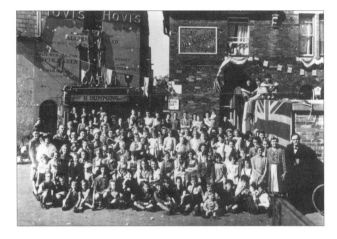

*Another special occasion in Hope Square, with the Union Jacks and bunting, plus what appears to be an air-raid shelter on the right, suggesting that this is a VE Day celebration in 1945. Dunning the Baker, on the left, is now an antiques shop. Following a late-twentieth-century trend for revamping pubs and changing their names, Hope Square's Red Lion became for a few years The Dorset Brewers Ale House, but has now thankfully reverted to its original, short and best-remembered name.*

*German bombs badly damaged Devenish's Brewery on 11 August 1940. Rival brewer Groves assisted with the company's production following the air raid, and above we see the devastation caused in the attack and the buildings as they are today.*

# Hope Street

*Hope Street, c.1880*

Late in the 1880s the Great Western Railway took over the ailing Weymouth & Channel Islands Steam Packet Company and introduced three large new steamships on the cross-Channel service. These new vessels, the *Lynx*, *Antelope* and *Gazelle*, needed more space to swing around in Weymouth Harbour and to provide it, this row of cottages on the east side of the cove was demolished and a new quay wall constructed. Some two-thirds of the area where the cottages stood is now beneath the waters of the harbour. These were the backs of the houses, some with direct access to the water: their front entrances were in Hope Street.

*Hope Street, 2003*

Prior to their demolition, the old cottages completely obscured properties on the east side of Hope Street. Today the occupiers of this row of houses (Nos 16–24 Hope Street) enjoy harbour views thanks to the requirements of the GWR ships over a century ago.

*Just a short walk beyond the Cove are the steps which lead down to one of Weymouth Harbour's most delightful holiday-season attractions. For just a few pence the ferry boat carries its passengers across the harbour to disembark close to Devonshire Buildings – and where there is usually a queue waiting to be rowed to the other side. When the Condor Wavepiercer craft are in harbour the brief ferryboat trip offers an unusual view from the waterline of these huge high-speed vessels.*

*A second view of the old Cove properties prior to their demolition shows Weymouth Barracks in the centre background. Usually known as the Red Barracks, these were originally built in 1795 as Cavalry Barracks but they were rebuilt in 1800 following a serious fire, after which they accommodated 17 infantry officers and 270 men. They date from a lively period in Weymouth's military history. The country was at war with France, and King George III and his family were spending long summer holidays in the resort, with an ever-present threat of invasion from across the Channel. This was one of three Georgian barracks in Weymouth which, with tented camps around the town, accommodated many hundreds of soldiers. By the 1980s the Red Barracks had fallen into disuse and there was a real fear that they would be demolished, but these historic buildings have now been very successfully converted to housing.*

# Inner Harbour 1

*Inner Harbour, 1960s*

This Inner Harbour scene dates from forty years ago, and illustrates well Weymouth's transport of yesteryear. Stretching across Radipole Lake in the background is the steel viaduct which carried the Weymouth and Portland Railway from Melcombe Regis Station to Westham. The last scheduled trains ran on the line in 1965 and the viaduct was removed in the mid-1970s. Vessels tied up alongside Cosens' marine engineering works in Commercial Road include two of their own paddle-steamer fleet and the *Vecta*, belonging to Cosens' parent company, the Southampton, Isle of Wight & South of England Royal Mail Steam Packet Company Ltd., and probably in for a refit. As can be seen by the line of wagons on the Ferry's Corner siding, the Weymouth Harbour Tramway was in regular use at this time.

*Inner Harbour, 2003*

Since 1989 a road bridge has taken traffic across Radipole Lake, almost following the line of the old railway viaduct. Pleasure craft now fill the Inner Harbour south of Westham Bridge, and since Cosens left their works on Commercial Road in 1987 no larger vessels have passed through the Town Bridge for repair or winter laying-up. Cosens' workshops and many other buildings along Commercial Road were demolished in the 1980s and the area was subsequently redeveloped as a shopping precinct and, as can be seen here, apartment blocks.

*These buildings alongside the steps at Chapelhay would have enjoyed the same views across the harbour, but they, like so much of Chapelhay, suffered bomb damage in the Second World War and were demolished. Pre-war shops on this high ground above North Quay were Amos, who had two shops, a dairy and a tobacconist, and Gardner the fruiterer. After the Municipal Offices were built on the North Quay site this area behind them was walled off and planted out as a small garden, from where the 2003 photograph of the harbour was taken.*

*Almost directly below the Chapelhay shops stood No. 4 North Quay, lost in postwar years despite strenuous efforts to preserve it. Weymouth's harbourside Tudor House was demolished in the 1960s, as were many neighbouring properties, to provide the site for the Municipal Offices (opened in 1971) and its car parks. Not far away, at 2 and 3 Trinity Street, near Hope Square, Tudor houses do still stand. Cared for by the Weymouth Civic Society, they are open to members of the public at advertised times.*

# Inner Harbour 2

*Inner Harbour, 1950s*

Taken from the Town Bridge, probably in the late 1950s, this view looks along North Quay towards the Sidney Hall and Weymouth football ground, with the embankment of the Weymouth and Portland Railway seen behind them. On the left, buildings along North Quay would be razed within a few years of this photograph being taken, to provide a site for Weymouth's Municipal Offices.  In the centre of the row is the historic Tudor House at No. 4 North Quay, which was demolished in 1961, with the Phoenix building (left) and adjacent garage following in 1965.

*Inner Harbour, 2003*

The scene in 2003 is much changed, with Municipal Offices on the redeveloped North Quay, and an Asda supermarket in place of the Sidney Hall and football ground – the supermarket and its car parks now totally fill these sites and, sadly, the large trees which once surrounded them have all disappeared.  The Sidney Hall was pulled down in 1987, and at the same time Weymouth Football Club relocated to an out-of-town site at Southill, where the stadium has as a neighbour the town's new Police Headquarters.  In front of the Municipal Offices can be seen the southernmost pontoons of the Weymouth Marina complex.  The large building on Westwey Road is a development of 1972 (Benefits Agency offices), alongside the white flat-roofed Magistrates' Court of 1978.

*Two views of Weymouth's Municipal Offices on North Quay: a 1969 view showing the girder work during construction (with the postwar flats on Chapelhay Heights visible behind), and a night-time view of the completed building – which was opened by HRH Princess Anne on 1 June 1971.*

# Inner Harbour 3

*Inner Harbour, 1974*

Although only some thirty years have passed since this photograph was taken of the Inner Harbour, the only prominent feature which is easily recognisable today is the gasometer on the far left of the picture; its neighbour was taken down in the 1980s. In the foreground is the

Victorian dam, an attempt in the 1870s to control the flow of the lake out to sea and thus maintain a minimum level in the lake's upper reaches. Many were the complaints about the smell given off when the mud was exposed. The dam also served to flush out the Inner Harbour, which could also become unpleasantly smelly as the town's sewage was pumped into it. These problems were partly overcome in the 1890s when a new sewage system with a sea outfall was begun, and further improved in 1921 when the present Westham Bridge was built, controlling the flow of water with sluices. In 1974 the scaffolded chimney of the disused Sunnybank electricity power station was being dismantled and in front of it, along Westwey Road, three buildings were to disappear before the end of the century – the St John Ambulance Hall, a pair of semi-detached houses and the ambulance station.

*Inner Harbour, 2003*

In 2003 the same view is much livelier. The dam's removal in 1995 was followed by the installation of pontoons providing plenty of accessible boat moorings, and more facilities were provided by the construction of a marina building on an adjacent site. Along Westwey stand a new St John Ambulance Hall (the old hall's crumbling foundations had made the structure unsafe), a probation hostel in place of the two houses and a motorcycle showroom on the site of the ambulance station (the service having transferred to Dorchester). Some of the trees are to be preserved by the developers of the land which lies behind them, on which formerly were the workshops and yard of Weymouth and Portland Borough Council. Apartments are under construction here, the WPBC works having relocated to Chickerell.

*A view from the western side of the Inner Harbour, with the dam on the right. The old Westham Bridge of the 1850s was wooden and originally had a central drawbridge, later removed. The spires of three churches are visible in the background, only one of which – St John's, on the far left – remains today. The chimney in the centre of the picture was that of a foundry off Park Street.*

*The electricity supply for the town was initially switched on in 1904, and until nationalisation in 1947, Sunnybank power station was owned by Weymouth and Melcombe Regis Borough Council. The local station was switched off in 1966, but it was 1974 before its chimney was taken down – brick-by-brick owing to the close proximity of neighbouring terraced houses.*

# John Groves Building, St Thomas Street

*John Groves Building, 1966*

In ornate Victorian style, this very handsome building stood on the corner of St Thomas Street and Lower St Alban Street and was the registered office, bonded store and off-licence of local brewer John Groves.

The company's brewery was located in Hope Square, alongside rival local firm Devenish, which eventually took over neighbour Groves in a 1960 merger. This photograph was taken in 1966, the year the buildings on this corner of St Thomas Street were demolished.

*John Groves Building, 2003*

The less attractive, but functional, 1960s architecture of the Tesco *Metro* store now fills the old Groves corner site, and its range of groceries and household wares is undoubtedly more appealing to the modern shopper – and supermarkets have taken on much of the off-licence trade. This particular *Metro* is reputed to have the highest turnover per square yard of floorage of any Tesco store. The barrier in the foreground is used today to close the centre section of St Thomas Street to traffic outside of specified delivery hours, thus daily turning it into a pedestrian precinct.

.THE OLD BANK, WEYMOUTH.

*Adjacent to John Groves' offices in Victorian times was Eliot, Pearce & Co.'s Old Bank, established in the town in the 1790s. Confidence in the firm was implicit and practically every local business and organisation banked at Eliot's. News of the Old Bank's failure in 1897 was a colossal shock, and the financial disaster affected towns and villages throughout south Dorset. In Weymouth large concerns such as Cosens, the gas and water companies, the Borough Treasurer and HM Customs banked at Eliot's, but the crash also caused great distress to individuals – working people who, wisely they thought, saved regular amounts there and children who were encouraged to save through school savings accounts. When the whole sorry affair was finally sorted out, the Old Bank's creditors received just 7s 11¼d (40 pence) in the pound. The old bank building was demolished in 1966, its site now forming part of the Tesco store.*

*Facing Tesco on the opposite corner in St Thomas Street is the post office, a handsome Edwardian building of 1907, later extended. Its predecessor had been just down the street in much smaller premises next to the Old Bank. There had been many complaints about the cramped conditions in the old post office, and it certainly must have been a little overcrowded in June 1891 when the local press reported the following incident: 'About nine o'clock on Wednesday morning as some bulls were being driven through St Thomas Street five of them went into the post office in a very quiet and orderly manner, much to the surprise of the officials, who were in a place of safety behind the counter. The animals were not at all frightened by their presence in the post office, calmly making an inspection of the bills containing the latest telegraphic notices and then, on the appearance of the driver, being driven out. Fortunately at the time, there were only one or two of the general public in the office.' (The reporter failed to note the customers' reaction to this bovine invasion).*

# Jubilee Clock

*Jubilee Clock, c.1920*

Fashions of the day suggest a date of around 1920 for this photograph of the Jubilee Clock. Erected to commemorate the Golden Jubilee of Queen Victoria in 1887, the clock is shown on its original stone promontory, built on the beach and reached from the sands by a flight of 12 stone steps. The clock tower was paid for by public subscription, but funds proved insufficient to purchase the clock mechanism for it to fulfil its intended purpose. The town then requested and obtained the gift of a clock from its wealthy former MP, Sir Henry Edwards, who represented

Weymouth in Parliament from 1867 to 1885. His generosity was well known, and continued after his twenty years at Westminster – where he had been known as 'Linseed Edwards', for some of his fortune had been accrued in the marketing of linseed. Once retired from politics, Sir Henry built and endowed homes for the aged on Boot Hill and in Rodwell Avenue.

*Jubilee Clock, 2003*

Later in the 1920s the Esplanade was widened out around the base of the Jubilee Clock tower, the project providing work for some of the men who had returned from fighting in the Great War to find widespread unemployment at home. Once completed, the promenade's broad sweep seaward was a great improvement on the former narrow walkway in front of the clock and the new extension helped to keep the shingle at the northern end of the beach from encroaching onto Weymouth's star attraction, its golden sands. The decorative coloured lights, seen attached to the clock tower, are rather bland and boring by day – but when illuminated at night dramatically emphasise the beautiful sweep of Weymouth Bay.

*The Jubilee Clock is extremely decorative and since the 1920s has been painted in gilt and bright colours in keeping with its seaside location. These panels not only record its unveiling, but remind us that John Groves, the local brewer, was the town's Mayor at that time.*

*The newly extended Esplanade. A view from the late 1920s.*

*On the sands below the clock, and providing countless children with gentle rides since Victorian times, were the Weymouth donkeys. This photograph of around 1910 shows the Wood children, Leslie and Eric, and is from the family's holiday photo album. Sadly, the donkeys no longer wait patiently on the beach – they retired, with their owner Mr Downton, in 2000. Each summer day, at teatime, the donkeys were taken home across the Town Bridge and along North Quay where they held up the traffic, but were such a delightful sight that no one seemed to mind.*

# King's Statue

*King's Statue, c.1880*

Commemorating King George III's association with Weymouth, the King's Statue, unveiled in 1810, stands at the entrance to the town's two main streets. This remarkably empty view of the area around the statue dates from the end of the nineteenth century. It was here that the local horse-and-carriage transport fleet would normally assemble, but the barriers in the roadway perhaps suggest that a special event was imminent, and that horse droppings would not be welcome underfoot! This large open space was once a popular venue for parades and celebrations and would be thronged with crowds on such occasions. The elegant street-level bow windows of the building behind the statue would eventually and almost inevitably give way to the plate glass of modern shop premises.

*King's Statue, 2003*

In 2003 the King's Statue is surrounded by gardens laid out in the mid-1950s on the large island around which today's traffic circulates. This has not always been a popular monument. From the original delays in getting the statue erected in the early nineteenth century there have been suggestions through the years for re-siting King George III – or even disposing of the statue altogether. None were proceeded with and the King continues to gaze upon the sea front where he spent fourteen long summer holidays between 1789 and 1805. Formerly painted in drab green or bronze, the present heraldic colours first decorated the statue in 1949 and are a much admired feature today. The King's Statue is now a Grade I listed building.

*A close-up of the detail atop the statue's Portland stone plinth.*

*Anyone for a day trip? Horse-drawn carriages wait for passengers at the statue in the early 1900s.*

*The use of the King's Statue area as a 'terminus' for the men who plied for trade in their horse-drawn cabs at the end of the nineteenth century led to the provision of the Tea Cabin on the sea front. Here they could obtain refreshments and shelter between journeys. An early proposal that the Tea Cabin should be run by a Temperance Society was rejected as it was felt that the cabmen would want 'a drop of beer' with their dinners. No drink-driving laws in the 1870s! The Tea Cabin is still in business, supplying holidaymakers and locals with cups of tea, ice-creams and the like to enjoy in the sunshine.*

# Littlefield Level Crossing

*Littlefield Level Crossing, 1960s*

This photograph from the 1960s looks from the platform of Westham Halt towards the level crossing at Littlefield in Abbotsbury Road. The Weymouth to Portland railway line operated for a hundred years, opening in 1865, closing to passengers in 1952 and to goods traffic in 1965. The signal box is on the right of the picture and the crossing keeper's cottage on the left.

*Littlefield Level Crossing, 2003*

In 2003 the track of the old railway has been taken up, but its route from Westham to Wyke Regis can be followed on foot along the Rodwell Trail, passing traces of the old stations and halts en route. The imposing gate pillars which denote its starting point are not 'railway memorabilia' – they were formerly situated at Castletown, Portland, close to the foot of the Merchants' Railway incline and at the entrance to the road which led to the old naval quarters. The pillars were 'rescued' when buildings were demolished in 1986 to make way for the present large naval accommodation blocks erected on the site. Although the large building on the right is now the headquarters of Betterment Properties Ltd, it was actually built for Lloyds Bank as an out-of-town business banking centre, but minimal use led to its closure at the end of 1996.

*Taken from the same direction as the photographs opposite, this view shows a crowded 'special' approaching Littlefield Crossing on 27 March 1965, the last day trains ran on the line. Following protracted discussions regarding the erection of a footbridge over the line at Littlefield, these proposals were dropped in favour of the subway shown here which opened in 1922. One motorist waiting impatiently for the train to pass decided to drive his car through the subway and was subsequently prosecuted and fined!*

*A short way along the 3-mile Rodwell Trail to Ferrybridge, the only place where walkers have to leave the old railway route is at Newstead Road, where the embankment bridge, seen here before demolition, took the line above the roadway. The bridge was taken down in 1987 to allow for road widening.*

# Littlemoor Road Junction

*Littlemoor Road Junction, c.1920*

This early-twentieth-century scene shows Littlemoor Road at its junction
with Dorchester Road. The house seen here, and known as 'The Corner
House', was demolished in the late 1970s when traffic lights were installed

and the road widened to accommodate the ever-increasing flow of vehicles between Weymouth and Dorchester. The wall in the foreground enclosed St Nicholas churchyard and, covered in rich foliage, it can still be seen today – although further back from the kerbside than before. Out of the picture to the left, on the opposite side of Dorchester Road, was the boot and shoe repair business of Edgar Hodges, who plied his trade there for over twenty years.

*Littlemoor Road Junction, 2003*

A rare traffic-free moment reveals the grassy knoll where the house in the old picture once stood, and the whole of the house beyond it (which is only partly visible in the top photograph) can now be clearly seen to the left. The bungalow in the centre is, of course, a more modern building. Edgar Hodges' shop at 641 Dorchester Road later became a gents' hairdresser's, and is now Classix, Ladies and Gents Hairdresser.

*Littlemoor Road in the 1920s, seen from a vantage point adjacent to the nearby railway station. The New Inn, with its distinctive entrance porch, is in the centre of the picture and, like the cottages on either side of it, is easily recognisable today. Most of the land in the foreground is now filled with the houses around Broadwey Close – but the skyline is unchanged, with the clump of trees on the Ridgeway still a prominent feature.*

*Further east along Littlemoor Road stood Thornhill Farm, which has long been demolished. The modern-style church of St Francis of Assisi was built where the farmhouse once stood, with the rest of the farmyard site now covered by properties built during a later phase of the development of Littlemoor, which had initially begun with the building of a dozen or so houses in Canberra Road between the wars. In the 1950s the expansion at Littlemoor took off, and today the area between Broadwey and Preston is one of Weymouth's major suburbs.*

# Lodmoor Airfield

*Lodmoor Airfield, 1920s*

Two hangars and some ancillary buildings, together with a passenger biplane, grace the far side of the Lodmoor airfield, as seen from a rather busy (by the standards of the time) Preston Road in the early interwar years. The airfield, on the site of former cricket, tennis and agricultural show grounds predated Weymouth's other airstrip at Chickerell, but came out of use much earlier – probably in 1935. This humble stretch of grass, now waterlogged, can claim a stake in aviation history, for it was here that Lieutenant Charles Samson landed his Short S38 seaplane after making the first-ever take-off from the deck of a moving warship – HMS *Hibernia*, in Weymouth Bay on 12 May 1912. In the interwar years the airfield saw a small amount of conventional passenger flights, both scheduled and charter, and the activities of a number of aerial circuses.

*Lodmoor Airfield, 2003*

The scene today shows ever-increasing numbers of vehicles using Preston Beach Road, and today all signs of the former airfield have disappeared, Lodmoor now being the site of an RSPB Nature Reserve – one of two in the town. (The other is Radipole Lake, a unique reserve in that it is surrounded on all sides by built up areas, yet has a marvellous range of species visiting it, either on passage, to winter-over or breed.) In times of stormy weather hundreds of tons of beach shingle were regularly hurled over Preston Beach wall, blocking the road and disrupting traffic. In 1995 a new wall, from which this photograph was taken, strengthened the sea defences and extended the promenade to Overcombe Corner – but the problems of shingle movement have still to be fully solved.

*Avro 504K G-EBLA at Lodmoor in the mid to late 1920s, with the hill beyond – although now covered with housing – readily recognisable. Tragically, on 19 June 1928 this aircraft crashed in Weymouth Bay whilst carrying out aerobatics, the pilot Mr A.C. Cooper receiving fatal injuries.*

*The Lodmoor Reserve is predominantly a grassland and salt-marsh habitat, with an extensive area of reed beds. Like the Radipole Lake Reserve, there are many species of birds present: waders, wildfowl, warblers, gulls and the like. Excellent bird-watching opportunities abound, both from the observation shelter and the paths which criss-cross Lodmoor.*

# Lodmoor Hill

*Lodmoor Hill, c.1925*

Its length, stretching away in the distance towards Radipole, reveals that this is a main road, but otherwise Dorchester Road could almost be a quiet tree-lined suburban avenue in this view taken around 1925. Buildings on the left were then substantial private residences, their front gardens walled and gates flanked with impressive entrance pillars. On the right can be seen the road's junction with Fernhill Avenue; the bus, soon to reach the stop at Radipole Spa, was one of the GWR fleet on a route which had been extended as far as Upwey in 1920.

*Lodmoor Hill, 2003*

Patience was needed in waiting for a break in the constant traffic using this main thoroughfare out of Weymouth to the county town of Dorchester before this shot could be taken in 2003. Business premises have taken over a number of the houses on the left-hand side; tarmac has replaced their former front gardens, and only one of the old gateposts has survived.

*Built in the mid-nineteenth century, the original Lodmoor House was converted to become a private school – later known as Lodmoor High School – and went on to become a guesthouse, then a nightclub and casino. By 1989, however, the Grade II listed building was abandoned and dilapidated and it was demolished. One of the conditions of the rebuilding was that the facade of the new house should closely resemble the original – as indeed it does. Today's Lodmoor House is occupied by the Avon-Lea Residential Home. It stands on the apex of Lodmoor Hill.*

*The Lodmoor Hill area until late in the nineteenth century fell within the parish of Radipole, and it was here in Georgian times that Radipole Barracks was built, one of three barracks heavily manned during King George III's summer visits to Weymouth when there was a constant threat of invasion from French forces across the Channel. The barrack square was enclosed by the present Westbourne and Alexandra Roads. These buildings, once officers' quarters, survive in Radipole Terrace – shown here in 1968 – whilst the nearby Hanover Road is a reminder that the barracks once housed the Hanoverian troops of the King's German Legion.*

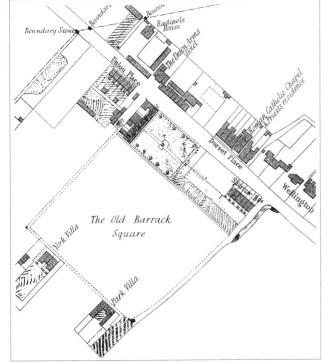

*The extent of Radipole Barracks off Dorchester Road, from Pierse Arthur's Map of Weymouth, 1859.*

# Lower Bond Street

*Lower Bond Street, 1988*

This was Lower Bond Street in 1988, leading from Commercial Road through to St Thomas Street. Bond Street's former name was Coneygar Lane, or Ditch, an indication that in the town's early history, when its houses clustered around the harbour, these were the outskirts of

Melcombe Regis with only isolated buildings to the north. Kennedy's builders' merchants occupy the foreground building, formerly the site of the Regent Garage Co. Before that Burdon's Buildings stood here, an overcrowded tenement block in converted Georgian barrack buildings. Up the street were two pubs – the Lamb and Flag, closed in the 1950s and converted to Aggie Weston's Royal Sailors' Rest, and the Golden Eagle.

*Lower Bond Street, 2003*

Starting in 1989 large parts of the very centre of Weymouth were either demolished (such as the Jubilee Hall) or boarded-up (such as whole of the north side of Lower Bond Street) in preparation for total redevelopment of the area. Various schemes fell through and for a while it was little more than a series of car parks and neglected areas resembling bomb-sites. One of the plans finally came to successful fruition in 2000 with the complete rebuilding of the cleared ground. Thus in 2003 the scene is difficult to replicate exactly, as Lower Bond Street (now renamed New Bond Street) has been pedestrianised and the former junction with Commercial Road is now just a narrow pedestrian passageway.

*The White Hart on the south side of Lower Bond Street dates from the early seventeenth century and was once the house of Sir John Browne, a wealthy merchant of the period. It is traditionally thought to be the birthplace of the famous painter Sir James Thornhill. The historic listed building is the lone survivor of the Bond Street redevelopment.*

*This very rare picture is of thelarge Georgian barrack block – the Queen's Barracks – on what is today the junction of New Bond Street and Commercial Road, and where Kennedy's store once stood. Few pictures of the barrack block exist. It was demolished late in the 1920s, having become known as Burdon's Buildings, a tenement which housed many Weymouth families. In 1925 it was declared unfit for human habitation (it was described as a plague spot) but nothing was done to rehouse its occupants. For two years they faced eviction and during a rowdy meeting at the Guild-hall demanded new homes from the council. Eventually some of the tenants were given houses on the council estates at Westham.*

# Maiden Street

*Maiden Street, c.1920*

The junction of Maiden Street and St Edmund Street was known for years as 'Hurdle's Corner', taking its name from the grocer's shop which stood here. Hurdle's had other shops around the town and were also pork butchers, with a slaughterhouse in St Nicholas Street. A pair of ancient and picturesque cottages adjoined the shop in Maiden Street, but they were demolished in the 1920s. The cottages appear in a painting by the noted English watercolour artist Thomas Girtin (1775–1802) which is now in the Victoria and Albert Museum.

*Maiden Street, 2003*

'Hurdle's Corner' with a twentieth-century extension where the old cottages stood, has been converted to a restaurant and bar since Hurdle the grocer gave up trading here in the late 1960s. Originally 'Captain Bonker's Bistro' this is now 'The Mariners'. Apart from changes in use, the adjacent buildings are easily recognisable in 2003. The rear wall of St Mary's Church is in the background.

*The seventeenth-century building on the opposite corner to Hurdle's has a cannonball firmly embedded in its wall, the damage being done during the town's hectic participation in English Civil War fighting in 1645, each side of the harbour for a time being held by opposing Royalist and Parliamentary forces. The cannonball probably dates from a Royalist attack on Melcombe in February 1645 when a barrage of firepower from the higher ground of Weymouth rained down on the town, setting fire to many properties. Below the cannonball can be found the doorway into this historic building's modern-day purpose: a public convenience.*

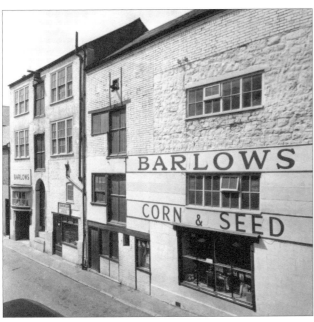

*These two Maiden Street buildings, now converted to bar and restaurant premises (Verdis and The Porthole) were for many years occupied by Barlows' corn and seed merchants.*

# Market House, St Mary Street

*Market House, 1957*

An interesting line-up of vehicles is parked outside the Market House in this 1957 view of St Mary Street. Behind the Ford saloon in the foreground can be seen a Vauxhall Velox and an Austin A30. The Market

House was the rather austere replacement of an ornate Victorian building which stood here until 1939. Its arched end wall survived demolition and was incorporated in this row of five shops with a central passageway through to Maiden Street. Trading in 1957 were (from left) Richard Shops (ladies' fashions), J. & M. Stone (radio dealers), Coopers (outfitters), K. Seal (evangelical booksellers and stationers), and the South Coast Furnishing Co. All have different occupants today, but a sign above the passageway – 'Camera Corner. In the arcade' – drew attention to a photographic business which still trades here under the same name forty-six years later.

*Market House, 2003*

No cars in 2003, for St Mary Street was pedestrianised in 1987. The planting of trees and flowers and provision of benches have since transformed the street scene. In recent years the Market House has undergone a complete transformation, its first floor having been converted to housing and its façade attractively modernised, after which the building was renamed Brenda Dench House in memory of Councillor Brenda Dench, Weymouth's popular Mayor in 1994 who very sadly died during her year of office.

*An artistic display inside the old Market House by green-grocer and fruiterer G.J.W. Denning, with a fine selection of fresh fruit and flowers available to the discerning purchaser.*

*This was the original Market House, built in 1855 and demolished in 1939, at a time when 'indoor shopping centres' seemed to go out of fashion. The pair of photographs probably dates from the mid-1930s, and trading inside at that time were assorted small shops and stalls including the two confectioners, Chick & Roberts; Dennings' greengrocery; Sams, the toy dealer; grocer Rashley; Watts, the dairyman; Holloways, fruiterers; and R.M. & A. Sheppard, nurserymen. Mrs Gertrude Forbes ran the refreshment rooms, Jesse Gosling collected the market tolls and John Lazarus was the premises inspector under the Shops Act. The finely detailed stone carving on the Weymouth and Melcombe Regis coat of arms was high above street level on the front of the old Market House.*

# Marquis of Granby, Chickerell

*Marquis of Granby, 1978*

In its original location the first Marquis of Granby pub stood opposite the end of Lanehouse Rocks Road, at its junction with Chickerell Road. John Manners, Marquis of Granby and Commander-in-Chief of the British Army in the late 1760s, gave his name to any number of English inns. But why are there so many 'Marquis of Granby' pubs scattered around England? The Marquis was very generous to wounded veterans of his campaigns and gave many of them bonuses when they were invalided out of army service – with which they purchased public houses and named them after their benefactor. Despite, or maybe because of his generosity, he himself died in debt! The old 'Marquis' is seen here shortly before demolition in 1978, and in the background can be seen the framework of a building that was then under construction – Weymouth District Land Registry.

*Marquis of Granby, 2003*

The replacement pub was built on a site to the north of the old 'Marquis' and the new pub's garden area stands where bricks and mortar once reigned supreme. Originally reopening as the 'Marquis of Granby', the chalet-style building was for a time, known as the 'Swiss Cottage', but in the 1990s it reverted to the 'Marquis of Granby' name – appropriately, since the area has been known for generations as 'The Marquis'. The large building in the middle distance is the Land Registry, with a feeder road in front of it (Cumberland Drive) leading off the main B3157 Chickerell Road into the Granby Industrial Estate. The estate, Weymouth's major light industries complex, occupies the site of the former Chickerell Airfield.

*The story goes that during a cavalry charge in 1760, soldier Granby's wig fell off during battle and pub signs ever since have portrayed him with an exaggeratedly bald head.*

*A contrast in styles: the 1878 Marquis of Granby, which lasted for a hundred years, and its successor built in 1978.*

# Melcombe Regis Station

*Melcombe Regis Station, c.1920*

An evocative sign on the platform informs the traveller *MELCOMBE REGIS STATION FOR PORTLAND TRAINS*. Here passengers waited for the trains that would take them over the viaduct which spanned Radipole Lake, then through Westham, Rodwell and Wyke to cross another bridge over the waters at Smallmouth before reaching Portland where a wonderfully scenic route took them to the top of the island – with the line ending at the Easton terminus station actually facing north! The Weymouth and Portland Railway opened in 1865 and carried its last regular passengers in 1952. This view was taken around 1920, before the huge infilling of the lake adjacent to Commercial Road began later in that decade, and shows an Adams O2 loco at the head of its train.

*Melcombe Regis Station, 2003*

In 2003 nothing at all recognisable remains from the scene of more than eighty years ago. This photograph is taken from outside the Commercial Road entrance of Weymouth Bus Station and shows the big apartment complex – Swannery Court – the construction of which in 2001 obliterated all trace of the old Melcombe Regis Station platform, by then the last visible reminder here of the line to Portland. The viaduct which took the line across Radipole Lake was dismantled in the mid-1970s, and in 1986 a road bridge took its place. The infilling of the 1920s had long ago reclaimed the land where the mute swans in the earlier picture hopefully awaited offerings of food from passers-by.

*At the end of King Street, at its junction with Commercial Road, this old pub – The Portland Railway Hotel – on the corner of Alexandra Terrace was to keep its name for quite a few years after the railway closed, before becoming the Dog House – proposals for a change of name to the Oar House having been firmly rejected! No longer licensed premises, the building has been converted to housing.*

*Melcombe Regis Gardens were laid out on the land reclaimed from Radipole Lake in the 1920s, and the Rose Walk was an attractive feature of them. Melcombe Regis Station cannot be seen in this postcard view from the 1940s, but the first span of the five-arch viaduct that once took the line across the lake is visible in the background.*

# The Nothe

*The Nothe, 1880*

The name of the photographer who captured this view more than 120 years ago is unknown, but the print is dated 26 June 1880. It is taken from the high up on the Nothe ramparts, and shows the pier very much as it looked after extensions of the 1840s. It was to remain little changed in shape until a major rebuild in the early 1930s, apart from a small extension which was reclaimed on the bay side to provide a site for the first Pavilion Theatre in 1908. In this picture there are few structures on the pier itself, apart from a rather basic landing stage which was replaced in 1889 by the Great Western Railway's new passenger facilities and baggage hall when the GWR took over the cross-Channel service from the rival Weymouth & Portland Steam Packet Company. The paddle-steamer at the pier is Cosens' *Premier*, which was to become the 'grand old lady' of the company's fleet – starting service at Weymouth in 1859, and remaining until she was scrapped in 1938. On the left of the picture is Devonshire Buildings; this terrace and the adjoining Pulteney Buildings were built early in the nineteenth century on reclaimed land at the southern end of the Esplanade.

*The Nothe, 2003*

Pier extensions in the 1930s were followed by a massive enlargement of the structure in the 1970s and 1980s, mainly to facilitate the unloading and parking of imported cars transported to the port on Ro-Ro ferries, and now used by travellers to and from the Channel Islands. Lorries carrying tons of waste stone from the Portland quarries to use as infilling made endless trips to the pier, leaving the roads they travelled covered with a film of white dust. Several huge Condor Wavepiercer craft often dominate this scene – these are the high-speed vessels which now oper-ate the cross-Channel service. On this day, one was in harbour – the *Condor Vitesse*, on the left of the photograph.

*The elegant Devonshire Buildings and Pulteney Buildings stand on land reclaimed from the sea in 1805, the terraces forming a dividing line which separates two very different facets of Weymouth's history. The front view from these bow-windowed houses is of the bay and promenade, reminders of the Georgian age when Weymouth found fame as royalty's favourite seaside resort. At the back, the view is of the harbour and recalls a much earlier time when trade through the port was the town's lifeblood. The picture dates from 1967 and the crane on the cargo stage is today just another part of Weymouth's history.*

*During what has become known as the 'Great Gale' of 23–24 November 1824, huge seas caused extensive damage to Weymouth's Esplanade and piers. An inscribed stone set in the wall of one of the raised flower-beds on the promenade commemorates this terrible storm when huge waves battered communities on the South Coast, destroying property, drowning inhabitants at Portland and virtually demolishing the little parish church at Fleet. The force of the sea can never be underestimated and its power was clearly demonstrated during severe gales in 1978 when waves crashing onto the stone pier at the southern entrance to Weymouth Harbour caused the damage shown here.*

# Nottington House

*Nottington House, c.1905*

Off Nottington Lane, and completed in 1817, Nottington House was an elegant Georgian mansion set in extensive grounds. For well over a century it was the home of the Tucker Stewards, a family which had great influence on business and politics in Weymouth in the eighteenth century. The house was built for Colonel Richard Augustus Tucker Steward, and was handed down through the family until inherited by Charleton Lochinvar Gordon-Steward in 1930, the last of the family to own Nottington House – and around this time it was sold. On the outbreak of the Second World War the Anti-Aircraft Gun Operations Centre for the whole of the County of Dorset was located at the Red Barracks, on the Nothe above Weymouth Harbour. However, in 1941 a new GOC became operational at Nottington House, with responsibility for the west of the county, with a second new GOC at South Lytchett Manor, near Poole, co-ordinating defences further east.

*Nottington House, 2003*

Desperate for accommodation in the post-Second-World-War years, the borough housed some families in wartime Nissen huts which stood in the grounds of Nottington House, but these were condemned as unsuitable in the 1950s and later demolished. The old house, meanwhile, was falling into decay and although it was understood that developers would convert it into flats, Nottington House was demolished in 1967. Nottington Court, the large apartment block which now stands in the grounds, was built 150 metres north-east of the original house, traces of which can still be seen – and the large tree on the left of the old photograph still exists.

*These stone pillars, seen here in the 1920s, no longer grace the entrance to the Nottington House site, although the fine heraldic carvings of vulning pelicans atop them have been preserved.*

*Controlled from the Second-World-War GOC at Nottington House, the main heavy anti-aircraft weapon in use in the local area was the 3.7in HAA gun – as seen here today on the ramparts of the town's excellent Museum of Coastal Defence at the Nothe Fort. Lighter 'point defence' weapons included the versatile 40mm Bofors gun – an example of which can also be seen at the museum. Note also in this picture the brazier, which is lit on numerous occasions for celebration or commemoration and clearly visible along the whole of the sea front and as far away as the Purbeck hills.*

# Old Town Hall

*Old Town Hall, c.1890*

Weymouth's Old Town Hall in High West Street dates from the days when the local government of the two towns of Weymouth and Melcombe Regis was administered quite separately. Melcombe Regis had its own town hall on the opposite side of the harbour and these two small ports at the mouth of the River Wey argued endlessly and acrimoniously over the profits from the trade of the harbour they were forced to share. Not until 1571 did the ministers of Queen Elizabeth I, weary of being called in to sort out the differences between the towns, enforce the union of Weymouth and Melcombe Regis into one borough, although it was still some years before real co-operation between them actually began. The attractive Old Town Hall dates from Tudor times, but rebuilding in the eighteenth century and extensive Victorian 'restoration' have obliterated most of its early features. Set on high ground above North Quay it is a picturesque landmark and reminder of local government of long ago.

*Old Town Hall, 2003*

Houses in High West Street can easily be identified in 2003, and railings added along the high pavement must be a welcome safety feature. In the distance is the modern and rather characterless architecture of the building which is the town hall of today for Weymouth and Portland Borough Council, the successor authority in 1974 to the former Borough of Weymouth and Melcombe Regis. Local government has transferred from one side of the borough to the other and back again. When the Guildhall in Melcombe's St Edmund Street was opened in 1838 it took over as the borough's administrative centre. The next location for borough council staff was the former Sanatorium in Clarence Buildings on the Esplanade, where they worked in very overcrowded offices from 1904 until 1971. Then it was back across the water to the current North Quay site, only a few yards from Weymouth's Old Town Hall.

Below the wall which runs along High West Street stood the Town Pump, installed in the 1770s to provide the Weymouth side of the town with a water supply – piped water was not available here until well into the next century. When first built it was situated amidst the houses of West Plains, Silver Street and Jockey's Row. Some of these terraces can be seen in the back-ground, with others having already been cleared to provide the site for Weymouth Fire Station at the foot of Boot Hill. When the fire station was built in 1939, the new building practically obscured the stone pump from public view, but in the 1990s it was decided to dismantle the pump and re-erect it near to Hope Square, where it can be seen more easily and appreciated as a once vital part of the history of the town.

*The Old Town Hall has had a number of occupants over the years and was regularly used as a polling station. Here a small crowd has gathered to hear the result of an election in the early 1900s, with Tett the Baker's delivery boy having temporarily abandoned his cart (left) to listen.*

# Outer Harbour

*Outer Harbour, 1914*

Tied up alongside the quay at Trinity Road in this 1914 photograph we see the twin-funnelled paddle-steamer *Monarch*. She was the first of Cosens' paddle-steamers to bear the name and was in service from 1888 until she was scrapped in 1950, her successor joining the fleet in 1951 until she, too, went to the breakers in 1961. The two lifeboats forward of the funnels (cream in colour with a black top-band) were extra boats added to conform with Board of Trade regulations imposed after the loss of the RMS

*Titanic* in April 1912. Across the water Great Western cargo vessels can be seen alongside the cargo stage on Custom House Quay, whilst clearly visible on the skyline is the chimney of Templeman's Crown Flour Mills, located at the junction of Helen Lane and East Street. The mills, established in 1892, supplied most of the local bakers and sent flour to other towns throughout the South West. They were burnt out in a huge fire in December 1917. Eighty-four years later, the tall building to the left of the mills, Maiden Street Methodist Church, also fell victim to fire, both blazes having begun early in the morning and taking a serious hold before they were detected.

*Outer Harbour, 2003*

The loss of both Templeman's Mill and the Methodist church result in a much lower skyline in the 2003 view. The large quayside warehouse on the left of the old photograph, usually known as the 'Red Warehouse', was demolished towards the end of 1958 and its site is now filled with extensions to the Ship Inn. Sadly, Cosens' paddle-steamers have also been confined to history – the last paddler, the *Embassy*, leaving port in 1967. Custom House Quay has fewer vessels alongside than is normal, with the converted lifeboat bearing the registration WH52 shown in the 1914 picture now also a memory. The railings in the foreground of both photographs have now been extended, but interestingly a lifebelt is still at the ready in the same position all these years later.

*Here we see a picture of Cosens' PS Victoria at Lulworth Cove, taken from one of the company's advertisements which were always included in the local guidebooks and highlighted pleasure trips to sea in the vessels of their fleet.*

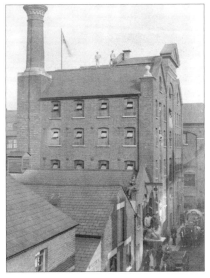

*Posing for a photograph in the early years of the twentieth century often involved a complete disregard for health-and-safety considerations. Here it appears that every man of the Templeman's Mills workforce was determined to be in the picture, and they probably had to remain in their precarious positions for quite a while until the time exposure was complete. Following the blaze which gutted the building in 1917, its chimney and upper floors were taken down, and the remaining outer walls on the corner of East Street and Helen Lane were later used in the conversion of the former mill into flats.*

# Overcombe

*Overcombe, 1970s*

From the 1970s, a view taken from the high ground above Overcombe Corner clearly shows the instability of the cliffs on this part of the coast. The chimney on the right belongs to a row of Coastguard cottages, once six in number, which stood on Furzy Cliffs below the Embassy Hotel (now renamed the Spyglass). No. 6 slipped down the cliffs in 1970. Further slippages, massive cliff protection works carried out in the early 1980s and the complete redevelopment of the area have now reduced the cottages to two properties. The beach groynes attempted, unsuccessfully, to hold back the power of the waves.

*Overcombe, 2003*

The cliff erosion makes it impossible in 2003 to regain the same photographic vantage point, but here looking towards distant Weymouth we can see the full extent of the new Preston Beach sea wall, the removal of the groynes and recent development at the foot of Bowleaze Coveway where it joins Preston Road. The large apartment block, with fantastic views seaward and across the nature reserve, dominates the centre of the scene and is known as Overcombe Court.

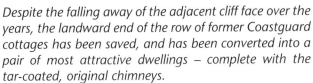

*Despite the falling away of the adjacent cliff face over the years, the landward end of the row of former Coastguard cottages has been saved, and has been converted into a pair of most attractive dwellings – complete with the tar-coated, original chimneys.*

*The Preston Beach Road toll-house was a relic of the days when it was obligatory to pay fees towards the upkeep of the highways before the gate was opened to allow traffic through. This little building is much better known as 'Sugar-em Shorey's', Mr Shorey having become almost a local legend. His family lived in the toll-house for around a hundred years, working as cabmen and log suppliers. Theories as to how he came by his 'Sugar-em' nickname abound, but one fact about his life is certain – Mr Shorey was a very unhappy man in 1959 when it was decided that his cottage was unfit for human habitation and had to come down. 'Sugar-em' did not appreciate his new council-house accommodation, with running water, electricity, heating and proper sanitation, 'luxuries' he had managed without all his life!*

# Pavilion Theatre

*Pavilion Theatre, 1910*

This 1910 shot shows in intricate detail the exterior of the old Pavilion Theatre, located at the entrance to Weymouth Pier. The Pavilion was opened with great ceremony by Lord Shaftesbury in 1908, and during the years of the Second World War acted as a headquarters building to both Royal Navy and United States Navy units operating from the harbour. It was retained by the military in the immediate postwar period for use as a sorting depot for parcels landed from RN ships, but once de-requisitioned it was refurbished and reopened, by now renamed as The Ritz, in 1950 – only to be gutted by fire four years later, a great loss to the local scene. The ornamental pier kiosk in the photograph survived the fire, but it was taken down when the present Pavilion was built. The elegant lady on the right is leaning against a notice indicating the direction to the Sailors' Home in the town, a reminder of the days when hundreds of naval ratings from HM and allied warships in Portland Harbour disembarked from liberty ships here for 'runs ashore'. The railway lines in the foreground carried passenger and goods trains along Commercial Road and Custom House Quay to the Harbour Station and to the goods-loading areas handling traffic to and from the Channel Islands.

*Pavilion Theatre, 2003*

The present Pavilion opened in 1960 and the photographer in 2003 almost inevitably finds a line of parked cars where there was once an open space. The railway lines of the Weymouth Harbour Tramway lie silent, and only the occasional special excursion train has passed over them since 1988. It was six years before this new theatre rose on the site of the old Ritz, following lengthy and expensive litigation regarding responsibility for the fire, and insurance and compensation claims. The Pavilion is a building very much of its time, its architecture not highly regarded forty years on. Attractive seashell and pebble panels with a seaside theme once enlivened the façade of the theatre, but years of south-westerly gales took their toll and the fragile artwork was eventually removed. It is a very plain face that the Pavilion presents to the town today, and the theatre may not survive if proposals first aired in the summer of 2003 for the redevelopment of the pier are adopted.

The blaze which destroyed the Ritz Theatre on 13 April 1954, the resort's largest postwar fire. The pier in front of the building is packed with people – as word spread that the Ritz was burning down, most of Weymouth turned out to watch, including both of this book's authors!

*When the fleet was in, Cosens' paddle-steamers were hired as liberty boats, ferrying the sailors to and from their ships in Portland Harbour. This photograph from the early 1900s shows four paddlers at the pier, very heavily and possibly overladen. Lifeboats were carried, but it was quite usual to find they could accommodate only a small number of those on board. Only in 1912 in the aftermath of the sinking of the RMS Titanic were the regulations regarding life-saving equipment on board ships strengthened and adhered to.*

# Penny Street

*Penny Street, 1908*

Weymouth's Park District houses were built on land which had been reclaimed from Radipole Lake in the mid-nineteenth century. The original plan had been to lay out an extensive public park with fine entrance gates and drives, but the scheme fell through and the intended parkland was used for grazing. When it was announced that the railway companies were extending their lines to Weymouth, and that land was required for station buildings and platforms, engine sheds and railway track, a sizeable area of the 'park' was sold to them in the 1850s. The remainder was bought in the 1860s by the Conservative Land Agency, a company which began building the terraces of what would become known as the Park District. Although reclamation had supposedly been completed, the drainage of the area was unsatisfactory, and in later years those who lived here would be plagued in wet weather by flooding. This photograph shows the junction of Hardwick Street and Penny Street under water in October 1908 following a heavy downpour.

*Penny Street, 2003*

Apart from a lack of flood water, the scene in 2003 is little changed, with the drainage problems in the Park District having been finally solved in the latter half of the twentieth century. Hardwick House (on the right) retains its distinctive patterned brickwork. The narrow streets and frequent road junctions were a source of modern traffic problems never envisaged by the Victorian developers of the area, but traffic calming measures and parking restrictions have now been introduced to improve safety in this residential area to the north of the town.

*Another soggy scene from 1908, this time looking down Hardwick Street from its junction with Derby Street.*

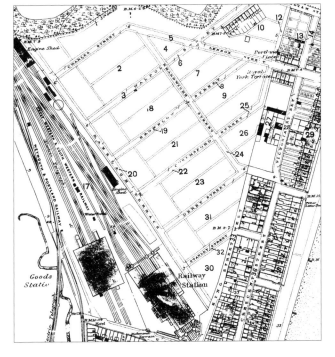

*The intended plan of the Park District was shown on the Ordnance Survey map of 1864. The grid layout of the streets behind Ranelagh Road (then called Ranelagh Terrace) is shown – the houses have yet to be built – with the backyards of the properties along each street being separated by alleyways. Between Charles Street and Walpole Street there were no plans at this time to include Penny Street, which was eventually built along the line of an intended passageway.*

# Preston Hill

*Preston Hill, 1950s*

Looking towards Weymouth from the eastern outskirts of the town, this
1950s scene would change only a little during the next fifty years – save
for the name of the public house on the main road through Preston,

which was then called the 'Ship Inn' (a Devenish house). Opposite the pub, close to the junction of Preston Road with Sutton Road, the front doors of old cottages opened directly onto the A353, but they were not to survive 1960s road improvements. The large sign on the corner advertised the Weymouth Bay Hotel (on the Esplanade at 6–7 Royal Terrace), and was a fixture here for many years.

*Preston Hill, 2003*

The 2003 view: on the left the nineteenth-century Ship Inn has been renamed the Spice Ship, but otherwise the scene has altered very little. On the other side of the road the demolition in the early 1960s of the cottages in the older picture allowed for some widening of this busy road out of Weymouth.

*This photograph shows that road widening had already begun on Preston Hill. Weymouth Council had applied for a demolition order on a house adjacent to this pretty thatched cottage in 1959, and in the early 1960s the cottage too was pulled down and its site lost under the tarmac of the present highway.*

*This cottage at Preston still stands south of the Spice Ship pub, but it is set back from the road and cannot be seen in the pictures opposite. Manor Cottage is an ancient structure, dating in part from the seventeenth century, and was once the home of John Wesley, grandfather of John Wesley the founder of Methodism, and his brother Charles, the famous hymn writer. Their father, Samuel Wesley, grew up in Preston, but had left the area before his sons were born.*

# RAF Chesil Bank Range Unit, Radipole Lane

*RAF Chesil Bank, 1950s*

The Royal Air Force Chesil Bank Range Unit opened in 1936, at Chickerell, on the site of one of the two former Weymouth airfields. Its function was to support the practice bombing and, for some of the years only, practice gunnery activities of RAF aircraft on the ranges in Lyme Bay and, for a while, actually on the Chesil Bank (Chesil Beach). As well as the support buildings, there was an airstrip here to enable the smaller aircraft using the ranges to land to refuel and rearm. Although the offshore ranges are still active, the support unit – known locally as RAF Chickerell – closed down in October 1959.

*RAF Chesil Bank, 2003*

Today all that remains from the military days is the concrete bellmouth leading off Radipole Lane in to the camp, where this small motor cruiser is regularly parked. The rest of the site is covered by an industrial complex, plus two residential streets: Cobham Drive, named after Sir Alan Cobham whose 'Flying Circus' staged events here in the mid-1930s, and Stainforth Close, commemorating the Weymouth-educated Wing Commander George Stainforth AFC, who gained the world airspeed record at 407.5 mph on 9 October 1931, following his earlier achievement in September of that same year when he first broke it. Sadly, he lost his life in North Africa in 1942 whilst commanding No 89 Beaufighter Squadron.

*During the spring of 1940 Westland Lysander Mk II army co-operation aircraft of No 613 (County of Manchester) Squadron were detached to Chickerell from their base at RAF Odiham in Hampshire to fly anti-invasion patrols off the Dorset coastline. This particular aircraft, L4799 seen in happier times, crashed in hill fog at Chickerell on 23 April whilst recovering to the airstrip after a sortie and short of fuel. Although both occupants escaped unhurt, the aircraft was a write-off.*

*Alf's fish and chip shop was popular with RAF personnel based at Chickerell and, after acquiring a taste for the traditional British fish and chips, USAAF personnel who were at Chickerell during the development phase of the American Tropposcatter Station at Ringstead. Prior to the base closure and the unit's relocation to Barrack Road, cadets from No 1606 (Weymouth) Squadron of the Air Training Corps were also regular customers. Today, Alf's continues as a popular 'port of call' for soldiers staying at the Army's nearby Wyke Regis Training Area, once known rather more descriptively as The Bridging Camp.*

# Radipole Lane

*Radipole Lane, c.1900*

A delightful summertime rural view as a pony and trap makes its way along Radipole Lane, towards St Ann's Church, the original manor house and the village school – beyond which lie the flood meadows of the River Wey as it meanders towards Radipole Lake, the harbour and its outflow in Weymouth Bay. In this view from around 1900, the building on the left is one of two lodges which originally stood at the entrances to Radipole's 'new' manor of the mid-Victorian period.

*Radipole Lane, 2003*

Would that such an idyllic rural scene was as easy to photograph in 2003! Even on a day in early spring, constant traffic speeding along this narrow stretch of road meant a patient wait before the photograph could be taken safely. The lodge, the southernmost of the pair and screened now by more trees than in the 1900 picture, is just visible on the left. The second lodge lies opposite the aptly named Manor Road, next to gate pillars at the main entrance to the Victorian Radipole Manor.

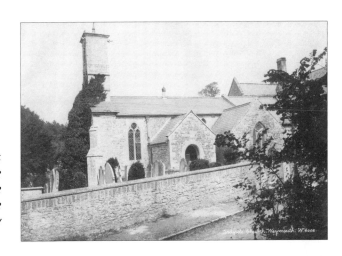

*St Ann's Church, in large part a medieval structure, was once the mother church of Melcombe Regis, the village of Radipole being of much older foundation than the harbourside development. The church's unusual triple bell turret is a distinctive feature, and was probably added in the seventeenth century.*

*The little Victorian former village school stands opposite the church and Old Manor. Built in 1840, it served the village children until the 1960s when the new Radipole County Primary School opened in Manor Road. Unlike many other closed village schools which have been converted to houses and other uses, the building still plays its part in the educational system, for it is now a playgroup and nursery school.*

*Next to the church is the original Radipole Manor, much of which dates from the sixteenth century. Weymouthians will recall one of its twentieth-century occupants, Mrs Iseult Legh, who was Mayor of the town in 1958 and active in many local organisations. Mrs Legh's husband, Commander A.J. Pennington Legh, DSC, RN, Retd. of the local Coastguard, was drowned off Chesil Beach in October 1944 in an heroic attempt to rescue the crew of an American landing craft LC(T)A 2454, manned by a Royal Navy crew, which got into difficulties in mountainous seas. Sadly another officer of the Wyke Coastguard, Mr R.H. Treadwell, and nine of the stricken vessel's crew were also lost.*

# Radipole Spa Bus Garage

*Radipole Spa Bus Garage, 1966*

The Southern National bus company's garage at Radipole, opposite the Spa Hotel, was originally built in the early 1920s for Road Motors Ltd., one of the earlier local bus operators.  Road Motors were taken over by the National Omnibus & Transport Company in 1925 and it was the division of the 'National' into three companies, Western, Eastern and Southern National in 1929 which brought the 'Southern National' name to Weymouth.  Other than the prominent name-board below the clock, the only other Southern National presence in the June 1966 photograph is the cluster of timetable boards between the two entrance doors, for none of the coaches on the forecourt belonged to 'The Southern'. The vehicle in the middle is a Wilts & Dorset MW coach, whilst flanking it on either side are a pair ex-Silver Star coaches, which passed to Wilts & Dorset ownership in 1963 as the result of a takeover. Just visible to the right is part of the Guy Toone car sales and repair garage, on the corner of Dorchester Road and Monmouth Avenue, with the company light-recovery Land Rover parked awaiting its next call to duty.

*Radipole Spa Bus Garage, 2003*

Southern National left these premises in 1970 and they were sold for business use. Three shops stood north of the garage. One is still a newsagents, its neighbour, Bignall's the Greengrocers, has been converted to a private house and the third, now an Indian take-away, is today more readily visible – for the public convenience block obscuring the view of them in the 1966 photograph has long been demolished. A number of businesses have been based at the old depot over the years; in 2003 the occupants are London Lounge, furniture retailers.

*A building which was associated with road transport long before motor omnibuses appeared in the borough was the toll-house at Radipole, a relic of the days of the turnpike trusts. It stood on Dorchester Road just south of the Spa, although the tolls were originally collected much closer to the town at a spot near St John's Church. In the nineteenth century the growth of the railways took away much of the road traffic and the trusts declined, their responsibilities eventually being taken over by the local authorities. The redundant Radipole toll-house was converted into two private dwellings, with windows facing directly onto the road, but it was demolished in 1972, this historic little building making way for road improvements. The heavy traffic which uses Dorchester Road today would make this an unbearably noisy spot to live, but one former toll-house resident recalled the endless stream of trucks and tanks thundering past it in 1944 during the build up to D-Day and in the weeks following, as thousands of American troops were brought from outlying camps to embark at Weymouth and Portland harbours. The little house shook, but not one of the heavy vehicles passing so close touched the building itself.*

*This snowy scene from the early twentieth century recalls yet another feature of the local transport scene which is no more, for trains once stopped at Radipole Halt. It was located directly behind the Spa Hotel, which can be seen in the background of this photograph, with the halt's pedestrian access to Spa Road on the left. Radipole Halt opened in 1905, the same year that the GWR began running a bus service from Wyke Regis to Radipole, an indication of the growth of two 'new' local communities at the end of the nineteenth and beginning of the twentieth centuries. Modern Wyke Regis had developed on either side of Portland Road following the opening of Whitehead's Torpedo Factory at Ferrybridge in the 1890s and 'new' Radipole was growing up along the Dorchester Road, away from the old village. A good indication of an expanding population is the opening of a new pub and the Spa Hotel opened in 1899. Today, although trains still pass the old halt, they no longer stop here, for it was taken out of service following BR's application in 1984 to close Radipole Halt owing to the poor condition of the platforms and the cost of repairing them.*

# Railway Dock Hotel,
# Rodwell Avenue

*Railway Dock Hotel, 1982*

The Railway Dock Hotel stood opposite the junction of Rodwell Avenue and Newton's Road and it was named in anticipation of a scheme which never materialised. In the late 1890s the Great Western Railway was finding Weymouth Harbour's facilities, although improved, still inadequate for the planned expansion of its steamer services. The GWR put forward plans to construct a new harbour inside the new Admiralty breakwater then under construction at Bincleaves, but when this plan was rejected, the company proposed a scheme to build a 56-acre (22.7 ha) dock with two jetties at Newton's Cove, the whole being sheltered by two specially constructed breakwaters. A new railway line some 4½ miles (7¼ km) long would leave the mainline at Upwey and swing round in a great bend west of Weymouth, thence through a tunnel under the Portland branch emerging near Castle Cove and making its way along Underbarn to the new port. The harbour scheme proceeded extremely slowly, the railway works were not begun at all and the ambitious plan was abandoned altogether in 1913. The name of the Railway Dock Hotel was practically all there was to remember it by and the pub was demolished shortly after this photograph was taken in March 1982, having been run by one family – the Underwoods – from the time that it was first built in 1902 until the tenancy changed in 1970.

*Railway Dock Hotel, 2003*

The demolition of the Railway Dock Hotel has provided a clear view of the houses in Newberry Gardens behind. Redevelopment of the lower end of Rodwell Avenue, Spring Road and Hope Square in the 1980s brought about the complete transformation of this area, with a blend of new housing and tourist attractions.

*This photograph of around 1905 shows Bincleaves breakwater and it was probably taken from near the only remaining reminder of the GWR's scheme for Newton's Cove – the railway-type footbridge over Newton's Road.*

*More than thirty years ago this old Great Western boundary marker – used to designate the limits of railway-owned land when cuttings, embankments, fences and the like failed to do so – could be spotted almost hidden in the hedge along Underbarn Walk, between Bincleaves and Sandsfoot Cove. It was a link with the Newton's Cove plan and showed that the GWR still owned the land in 1912, but it is long gone – lost either to one of the frequent landslips here or to a collector of railway memorabilia.*

# Rodwell Garage, Boot Hill

*Rodwell Garage, c. 1910*

Such a wonderful Edwardian scene, taken outside Bugler's Rodwell Garage on the west side of Boot Hill where Mr Bugler operated a taxi-service, and later charabancs, running trips to local beauty spots, towns and villages until 1916. His excursions then ceased until the end of the First World War and although he purchased vehicles after the war ended, he does not appear to have started up his business again to any great extent. He joined the Weymouth Motor Company as a director, but resigned, sold up his garage and moved away in 1920. The coats worn by the drivers are so very typical of those in fashion in these early days of motoring. The buildings on the extreme left and extreme right of the photograph are easily recognisable today.

*Rodwell Garage, 2003*

Boot Hill (officially part of Rodwell Road) in 2003. George Bugler's garage was in what was then known as 'The Rodwell Mews', and mews-style cottages have since been built on the site of the adjacent house to the south, facing into a yard where the garage once stood. Today it is difficult of imagine a fleet of taxis and charabancs regularly using this narrow, steep and busy hill. Garage proprietors Chantreys took over when Bugler left, the National Fire Service used the premises in the Second World War, and many locals will remember its postwar use as local department store V.H. Bennett's garage and workshops.

*Opposite the Netherton stand terraced houses of the late-Victorian age, homes built to accommodate the town's aged citizens and paid for by the local benefactor Sir Henry Edwards. This gift, made in 1894, was followed later by one of the cottage homes block in Rodwell Avenue, known as 'Edwardsville'.*

*On the hill just below the buildings shown in the photographs opposite is a substantial house dating in part from the seventeenth century and known as the Manor House or Netherton House – but better remembered in more recent times as the Netherton Hotel, its Plaza Toro restaurant in the 1960s said to be the first steak bar in Weymouth. The house's original owners, probably wealthy merchants trading through the nearby Weymouth Harbour, are not known, but it was the home of the Penny family from 1763 until the 1860s and continued to be used as a private residence until around 1960 when the house was converted to hotel use, and later used as a nursing home. A plaque now affixed to the wall outside commemorates the good deeds of one John Cree, of Osmington, who at his own expense paid for Boot Hill (then known as Boot Lane) to be widened in 1851.*

# Rodwell Station

*Rodwell Station, c.1910*

This 1910 photograph, taken from the overbridge in Wyke Road shows an 'up' train standing at Rodwell Station on the Weymouth and Portland Railway line. The line opened in November 1865, was closed to passengers in 1952 and to all traffic thirteen years later. Rodwell Station was positioned between Melcombe Regis Station and Wyke Regis Halt and boasted a fine garden, lovingly tended by the station staff. Rodwell, in 1870, was the first station to open on this stretch of the line, followed in 1909 by Melcombe Regis Station (trains had previously started their journeys at Weymouth Station), and Westham and Wyke Regis Halts. Sandsfoot Halt was of a much later date, opening in 1932. The Rodwell Station building shown here was destroyed in an air raid on 15 April 1941 which killed the only member of staff on duty, ticket collector Arthur Long.

*Rodwell Station, 2003*

Today the Weymouth Civic Society award winning Rodwell Trail follows the old railway line from Abbotsbury Road (former site of Littlefield Level Crossing and Westham Halt) to Wyke Regis. Although the old trackbed is now tarmacked for easier walking, traces of its railway history can be found all along the route. In 2003 platforms can just be glimpsed through the trees which have grown up around the Wyke Road Bridge – and these are all that remain of Rodwell Station.

*Emerging from the deep cutting where Rodwell Station was situated, the trains ran very close to the cliff edge as they headed along the shore of Portland Harbour towards Wyke Regis Halt. Landslips along here are not uncommon and this view of 15 January 1909 shows a sizeable slip near Sandsfoot which caused some disruption to services that day, passengers having to leave the train on one side of the slip and make their way on foot past the collapsed area to board another train waiting at the other side!*

*The start of the Rodwell Trail, opened in 2000 and part of the National Cycle Network, is marked by this information sign at its Littlefield Crossing end in Abbotsbury Road, and has proved very popular with local walkers and cyclists alike.*

# The Royal Oak, Upwey

*The Royal Oak, c.1905*

In a scene from a picture postcard of the early years of the last century, a horse-drawn caravan makes a sharp turn at the bottom of the hill at Upwey before starting the long haul up Ridgeway. On the corner stood the 'Royal Oak', a Devenish house, remembered by many later in the twentieth century not only as a popular pub but also as a bus stop. In those days the Southern National's No. 22 bus service from the King's Statue had two Upwey destinations, which alternated between journeys: 'Upwey Royal Oak' and 'Upwey Wishing Well,' both of which involved quite complicated reversing manoeuvres before the bus could return to the town.

*The Royal Oak, 2003*

In 2003 the cottages climbing up the old road in the background have changed little in almost a century, but the Royal Oak pub is no more. With ever-increasing road traffic at this dangerous and narrow corner, it almost inevitably made way for road widening in 1965. The sharp bend on which the Royal Oak stood was sliced away and today its site is lost under the modern roadway – where we see here a Wilts & Dorset double-decker bus passing the stop outside the old pub site, but in a non-standard colour scheme, for this particular vehicle is one of number nationally painted gold to commemorate the Golden Jubilee in 2002 of Her Majesty Queen Elizabeth II.

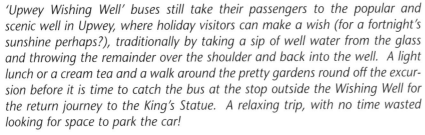

*'Upwey Wishing Well' buses still take their passengers to the popular and scenic well in Upwey, where holiday visitors can make a wish (for a fortnight's sunshine perhaps?), traditionally by taking a sip of well water from the glass and throwing the remainder over the shoulder and back into the well. A light lunch or a cream tea and a walk around the pretty gardens round off the excursion before it is time to catch the bus at the stop outside the Wishing Well for the return journey to the King's Statue. A relaxing trip, with no time wasted looking for space to park the car!*

*Today, the 'locals' at the foot of Ridgeway are the Royal Standard in Dorchester Road, and the old Ship located on the old 'Roman Road' over Gould's Hill, the main road serving Weymouth until 1824 when the present A354 replaced it. This is a road with easier gradients, but with a sharp hairpin bend at its junction with the turning to Bincombe.*

# Sandsfoot Castle

*Sandsfoot Castle, c.1900*

Now a picturesque ruin, Sandsfoot Castle was built in the reign of King Henry VIII and was one of a series of fortifications erected along the South Coast to defend the country from attack by sea. With Portland Castle, Sandsfoot was intended to protect Portland Roads, an anchorage for shipping long before the breakwaters were constructed to enclose

Portland Harbour in the nineteenth century. Portland Castle remains almost intact, but Sandsfoot started falling into disrepair almost from the time it was built, because of its situation so close to the cliff edge. By 1584 the castle, then only some forty-five years old, was being seriously undermined by the sea and repairs were put in hand. Although further works were carried out early in the seventeenth century and the castle was manned in the 1640s during the English Civil War, no further attempts were made to preserve it and Sandsfoot fell into decay.

*Sandsfoot Castle, 2003*

Viewed from its landward side, Sandsfoot Castle has changed little in the hundred or so years which separate these two photographs, although the fall of several tons of stonework onto the shore below altered its seaward face considerably in the 1950s. Generations of school-children scrambled over the ruins before the building was fenced off and many left their mark, for graffiti is nothing new and carved names and initials visible in the 1900 picture can still be picked out today, some dating well back into the nineteenth century.

*Until the 1930s Sandsfoot was surrounded by grounds given over to turf, on which stood a tea cabin, and at one time, a tennis court. In 1932 the Tudor Gardens were laid out, in keeping with the period of the castle and providing an attractive entrance from Old Castle Road. This draws large numbers of visitors to admire the gardens, the castle itself and the magnificent views across Portland Harbour to the Isle of Portland.*

*Sandsfoot Cove, seen here just before the First World War, lies just east of the castle and has long been a favourite spot for locals and holidaymakers alike. So, too, was Underbarn Walk, an attractive cliff-path stroll from the cove to the Nothe headland, but this is sadly now closed due to a succession of serious landslips on this unstable part of the coastline.*

# Shrubbery Lane, Wyke Regis

*Shrubbery Lane, 1890*

In 1890 a picturesque thatched cottage faced down Shrubbery Lane at Wyke Regis, with a row of thatched cottages on the left and the boundary wall of Wyke House on the right. It is the doorway of the house in the centre background of this old photograph which is the only link with Shrubbery Lane in the twenty-first century.

*Shrubbery Lane, 2003*

The picturesque thatched cottage which faced down Shrubbery Lane in 1890 was replaced in the early years of the twentieth century by Shrubbery Lodge, but still in today's picture is the old doorway. Its neighbour on the other side is a complete rebuild of a previous house on the site, much damaged when the scene here changed for ever on 28 June 1942, following an air raid in the early hours which completely destroyed the row of cottages in the 1890 picture, as well as Wyke's Old Ship Inn. Five were killed in the bombing. When postwar rebuilding took place, the road was realigned and the houses on the left of the road moved well back from the original building line, with a small grassed area being added in front of Shrubbery Lodge.

*Wyke House was an impressive Georgian mansion which stood nearby on land at the corner of Portland Road and Chamberlaine Road. Its extensive grounds, planted with trees and shrubs, extended as far as Shrubbery Lane, so may well have given the old thoroughfare its name. Wyke House was owned by the Swaffield family for more than a century, with the next owner, Harry Collingwood, converting the building to a residential hotel in the 1920s when it took the name Wyke House Hotel. Wyke House was demolished in 1974, the site remaining empty until the houses of Wooland Gardens were built on it in the 1990s.*

*The memorial we see here stands at the junction of Wyke Road and Portland Road, and was designed by Captain Francis Haigh, a Royal Navy engineer who worked at Whitehead's Torpedo Factory and lived at Wyke Castle throughout the First World War. Fifty-two Wyke Regis men – 42 Army and 10 Navy personnel – were killed in the 1914–18 conflict, and their names are on the obelisk beneath the words 'That right may prevail over might'. Most unusually, the memorial makes no mention of the conflict in which they died or gives any date information. Neither does it commemorate those parishioners who died in the Second World War; their names, both military and civilian casualties, are listed on a monument in All Saints' Church.*

# St Edmund Street

*St Edmund Street, c.1880*

From 1867 until 2002 Maiden Street Methodist Church provided a fine vista at the end of St Edmund Street, viewed here in the 1880s from its junction with St Thomas Street. The church has since been partially destroyed by fire, but apart from this the street scene was to change little in over a century. On the left is the Golden Lion Hotel, an old coaching inn with bay windows at first-floor level. The church occupied the site of another coaching inn, the King's Head, demolished in the 1860s. The porticoed Guildhall opened in 1838, the year of Queen Victoria's coronation. Not too much traffic about, but the bowler-hatted gentleman on the left stands beside a form of transport long gone from the local scene: one of the bath chairs used to take the elderly and infirm around the town. Note the window cleaners hard at work at the Golden Lion, with a second ladder erected beyond, and the ladder-carrying handcart parked at the kerbside.

*St Edmund Street, 2003*

Weymouth has some superbly placed churches. St John's Church spire is a stunning landmark at the end of Weymouth Esplanade and Holy Trinity provides an impressive view across Weymouth Town Bridge. Until 17 January 2002 Maiden Street Methodist Church's Victorian red-brick façade and rose window, which had made this view down St Edmund street so attractive, were intact, but the fire which ravaged the building that morning completely destroyed the church's interior, and this photograph shows all that is left of the once hand-some façade. The blaze was so intense that people living near the Grade II listed building were evacuated and burning debris showered onto vehicles parked beside it. In 2003, the handcart standing outside the butcher's shop on the right of the earlier photograph has inevitably been replaced by a parked car.

*Fire-fighters struggle to control the massive blaze at Maiden Street Methodist Church in January 2002, the rose window dramatically illuminated by the fierce flames.*

*An early photograph of St Edmund Street shows the Guildhall which in 1838 replaced an earlier town hall on the site and the King's Head Inn, where the shell of Maiden Street Methodist Church now stands. Today the Guildhall is best known as the site of the town's Registry Office.*

# St John's Church

*St John's Church, c.1880*

At the northern end of Weymouth Esplanade stands St John's Church, consecrated in 1854. This view shows the church in the 1880s, before all the infilling of the land at the top end of the Park District had been completed. This boggy area was just beyond William Street where the ground now drops away sharply from the higher level of the Esplanade. Dorchester Road runs behind the fence in the centre of the photograph. In the background between St John's Vicarage (left) and the church can be seen Greenhill House, overlooking the sea and later to become the Grand Hotel. The house on the right, Greenhill Lodge, also still stands today and has been converted to flats.

*St John's Church, 2003*

It is impossible to photograph the 1880s view from the same spot today as a row of houses – St John's Terrace – now stands on what was the empty foreground of the earlier picture. This shot was taken from the steps of Greenhill Lodge, on the opposite side of the road, looking towards St John's Terrace (Nos 3–35, Dorchester Road). The architect of St John's Church was Thomas Talbot Bury, who, as a young man, had worked on the detailing of the present Houses of Parliament buildings under Augustus Pugin and Sir Charles Barrie. Bury was the designer of many other church and secular buildings, which included Weymouth's Market House in St Mary Street and Holy Trinity School at Chapelhay (both now demolished). A rather hair-raising tale recorded in the St John's Church centenary history tells of three airmen ascending in a balloon from a nearby circus towards the end of the nineteenth century. Fearing that they would be swept out to sea, the crew operated the gas control valve too soon and the balloon dropped down onto the spire of St John's Church, where its ropes became entangled around the weather-vane. Frantic efforts by the airmen to free it were successful and the balloon eventually crashed on the beach at Greenhill, the three in the basket stepping out unharmed. The church weathervane fared less well and there were insufficient funds available to carry out immediate repairs!

*The statue of Queen Victoria stands in front of St John's Church and it was unveiled with great ceremony in 1902 by her youngest daughter, Princess Henry of Battenberg. Although Weymouth celebrated the Queen's Coronation and her golden and diamond jubilees in 1887 and 1897 with tremendous enthusiasm, the Queen herself had shown little interest in the town visited so often by her grandfather, King George III, and the statue simply commemorates her long reign of sixty-three years. Weymouth was on the itinerary during a tour she made as a fourteen year-old princess, accompanied by her mother the Duchess of Kent, and Victoria noted in her diary 'It is a pretty place and the houses are well built. It is very close to the sea and the sands are very fine'. In 1846, as Queen, she and Prince Albert paid another, albeit impromptu, visit to Weymouth when the Royal Yacht Victoria and Albert put into Portland Roads 'through stress of weather'. Queen Victoria, reported the local press, 'looked remarkably well'; a seasick Prince Albert 'appeared pale'. The 22-feet-high statue of the Queen was sculpted by George Simonds, and cast in bronze by J.W. Singer & Sons, of Frome.*

*Built as Greenhill House in the first half of the nineteenth century, this very fine private residence at Greenhill was to become the 'Grand Hotel' in the 1960s, as seen here, and its proprietor for many years was Edgar Wallis, Mayor of Weymouth in 1960. Now the wheel has turned full circle and the 'Grand' is once again in residential use, having been converted to apartments at the beginning of the twenty-first century.*

# St John's School

*St John's School, 1974*

St John's Church of England School served the children at the northern end of the town for more than a century.  Opened on 28 December 1864, the buildings were designed by local architect G.R. Crickmay and were intended to accommodate 230 boys, 253 girls and 158 infants – a total of 661 in what would be considered very overcrowded conditions by today's standards.  The school stood on the corner of William Street and Dorchester Road, opposite St John's Church – with which it had a very strong relationship.

*St John's School, 2003*

When closure was decided upon in 1974, the old school was put on the market as a redevelopment site for flats and garages – as we can see from the 'For Sale' sign on the wall in the older picture – and was demolished soon afterwards. The present residential St John's Court was erected on the site by local developer Mervyn Stewkesbury's Betterment Properties.

*Going ... going ... gone! This spectacular shot of the demolition of the old school's last remaining wall also provides a glimpse of Grange Road and the streets beyond.*

*In 1974 the children of St John's School transferred to these new purpose-built premises in Coombe Avenue off Dorchester Road, near Lodmoor Hill, and here we see some of the pupils lining up for the photographer prior to embarking on a 'keep fit' venture. In May 2000, when the New Bond Street shopping precinct opened, three eleven-year-olds from St John's Primary School – John Ackerman, Sarah White and Emma Dean – presented a time capsule on behalf of the school. This was buried alongside the plaque which is set into the paved area outside the new shops to commemorate the opening of the £28,000,000 development.*

# St Leonard's Church

*St Leonard's Church, 1950s*

The second half of the nineteenth century saw the great Victorian religious revival, and in a period of just fifty years no fewer than 14 places of worship were built in and around Weymouth. This was one of them, the Primitive Methodist Chapel of 1876 in St Leonard's Road at Chapelhay. Sixty-four years later Sunday School was in progress on the morning of 11 August 1940, when 58 German bombs fell across the borough. The Methodist church's organ was smashed and its windows shattered by blast and shrapnel. The minister, making his way to the scene, was astonished to find that none of the youngsters was hurt and that all the children were quite cheerful among the debris. Later that day he borrowed a blackboard, tied it to railings outside the building and chalked on it 'Give thanks to God, thanksgiving service tonight at 6.30 in the open air'. The chapel closed in 1962.

*St Leonard's Church, 2003*

With external characteristics somewhat similar to those of the old chapel, these flats – built in the late 1960s – now stand on the site at the junction of St Leonard's Road and Prospect Place.

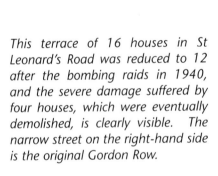

*This terrace of 16 houses in St Leonard's Road was reduced to 12 after the bombing raids in 1940, and the severe damage suffered by four houses, which were eventually demolished, is clearly visible. The narrow street on the right-hand side is the original Gordon Row.*

*This water pump once stood on Rodwell Road, close to its junction with St Leonard's Road. When erected in 1854 to supplement an earlier pump at the bottom of Boot Hill, it was outside the grounds of Springfield, the large house owned by the Devenish family, which has now been demolished (but its gate pillars can still be seen opposite the end of St Leonard's Road). The houses in the background of this 1963 picture – Portwey Close – have been built where the big house once stood. The Rodwell Road pump no longer exists; it was removed in the 1960s and is not the one which can be seen near Hope Square, which is much older and was originally sited behind Weymouth Fire Station.*

# St Mary Street 1

*St Mary Street, c.1900*

St Mary Street is seen here in about 1900, looking south towards its junction with Bond Street, once the site of the town maypole. The tall bank building on the right, No. 92, now occupied by Lloyds TSB, is easily recognisable. The tobacconist in the foreground offered American, Egyptian and Turkish cigarettes and outside the shop stood a gas street lamp. Most of the buildings on the left no longer exist. A lane runs alongside them, linking St Mary Street and New Street, known today as Blockhouse Lane, but appearing on at least one nineteenth-century map as Pope's Passage.

*St Mary Street 2003*

As to be expected in any main shopping street with the passing of a century, much has changed. A number of buildings on the right are still recognisable, whereas those on the left are less so – having undergone several major rebuilds since 1900. The latest development as a row of individual shop units dates from the 1980s, when the former Woolworth's store of 1938 was rebuilt.

*A late-nineteenth-century view of St Mary Street, looking north, shows the picturesque and ancient property that was replaced by the big bank building on the right-hand side of the pictures opposite. In the 1870s the occupant of No. 92 was Russell the umbrella maker and repairer, the shop sign topped with a delightful carved symbol of his trade. The two shops adjoining the lean-to beside Russell's shop can still be easily identified today.*

*F.W. Woolworth opened a large store on a site adjacent to Blockhouse Lane in 1938. The stylish cream-tiled Art Deco 'thirties' ocean liner' style façade is to some extent reflected in 2003 in the Spinnaker View apartments under construction at the foot of Boot Hill. Woolworth's left Weymouth in 1985, but returned in 2000 when the New Bond Street shopping precinct opened.*

# St Mary Street 2

*St Mary Street, c.1880*

This photograph of the lower end of St Mary Street was taken around 1880 and it shows one of the town's earliest buildings shortly before demolition. No. 45 St Mary Street stood on the corner of Church Passage, the lane which adjoins St Mary's churchyard and leads to Maiden Street. No. 45 was built in the sixteenth century and was pulled down in 1883. A few of its architectural details were preserved and built into the property which replaced it on the site. The milk churn mounted over the first-floor bay window of the next-door shop advertised that these were the premises of W.Hunt, dairyman and grocer.

*St Mary Street, 2003*

The building which replaced the Tudor No. 45 is occupied by gift shop La Luna in 2003, with a rebuilt Hunt's dairy at No. 46 now 'Treasured Memories', a gift shop with a nautical theme. The side door of No. 45's current premises in Church Passage is surmounted by a stone doorhead and brackets in the form of male and female figures which were saved from the old property. The railings which surround the churchyard can be seen in both photographs.

*St Mary's Church is the parish church of Melcombe Regis. The land on which it stands once formed part of the extensive medieval Dominican Friary which was founded in the town in the fifteenth century and closed in the Reformation during King Henry VIII's reign. The present church replaced an earlier, smaller church which by 1815 must have become a little dilapidated, as its ceiling fell down during a service. Today's St Mary's was designed by James Hamilton, local architect and builder in the Georgian period.*

*The altarpiece in St Mary's Church is 'The Last Supper' painted by Sir James Thornhill and presented to the town in 1721, and transferred from the original small church – where it had completely filled the end wall. Although Thornhill was history painter to King George I, knighted by the king and famous for his magnificent decoration of the interior of the dome of St Paul's Cathedral and murals at Greenwich Palace, information about his life is scant. He was probably born in Melcombe Regis, although his birth entry in the local parish registers appears to have been added at a later date. He certainly owned property in the town and was bound up in the extraordinary and corrupt politics of his day, representing the town in parliament from 1722. Thornhill also made a gift of some almshouses at the north end of St Thomas Street but having failed to endow them, the buildings subsequently fell into decay and were demolished, no trace of them remaining today.*

# St Nicholas Church, Buxton Road

*St Nicholas Church, 1964*

In the Southlands area of the town the green corrugated iron church of St Nicholas, known to locals as the 'Tin Church' or the 'Tin Tabernacle', was a familiar sight until it was demolished in 1964. Southlands at Rodwell had grown rapidly at the end of the nineteenth century and the iron church was erected in 1894 to serve as a temporary chapel of ease to Holy Trinity Church until a more permanent church could be built. The 'Tin Tabernacle' had already done good service in Salisbury until a new church replaced it there, and it was sold to Holy Trinity for £100 in 1894, with further costs of £110 to take it down, move it to Weymouth and re-erect on the Buxton Road site, plus £80 for furnishings and a harmonium.  St Nicholas Church was dedicated on 5 July 1894.

*St Nicholas Church, 2003*

Services were held in the 'temporary' church for seventy years and continued whilst a new permanent building was under construction on the same site in Buxton Road, just east of the 'Tin Church'.  Once the present church of St Nicholas was consecrated in the summer of 1964, the familiar corrugated iron chapel of ease was removed.  A second chapel of ease to Holy Trinity Church to serve the parish's population in the Pye Hill area of Chickerell Road was consecrated in 1908.  This was St Martin's Church, which has since closed and been converted to apartments.

*A close-up view of the present St Nicholas Church, Buxton Road, just visible on the right-hand side of the modern photograph opposite.*

*In the 1960s fairly drastic action was taken to widen the narrow T-junction at the meeting of Buxton Road with Rodwell Road and Old Castle Road.  A large slice of land was taken off the front garden of the corner house – No. 84 Rodwell Road  (shown here on the right) – and Buxton Road was widened along its north side as far as the bridge over the railway, beyond which is St Nicholas Church.  Many will remember the ruins of a house on this corner of Buxton Road, which had once been the home of local GP Doctor Scott.   His wife and three-year-old daughter were buried beneath the debris when enemy bombs demolished the building on 15 April 1941.  Both were rescued having suffered only minor injuries.  Their house had been surrounded by a pretty garden, and for many years afterwards roses and other flowers blossomed amongst its broken walls.  In the road widening of the 1960s the Scotts' old house was cleared and its site is now beneath the tarmac of the present roadway.*

# St Thomas Street

*St Thomas Street, 1954*

A view of the northern end of St Thomas Street illustrates the hazards of crossing the road here in 1954 when traffic was two-way in Weymouth's main shopping street and several bus routes terminated outside Frederick Place. A sizeable queue is waiting to board the No. 20 Chickerell bus. Although shop proprietors have changed, buildings on the left-hand side of the photograph are very recognisable today as their upper storeys are little altered. The large building in the centre of the picture was the 'Clinton', with an arcade of shops at street level and restaurant above. The arcade provided a welcome shelter for shoppers and holidaymakers on wet and windy days, and was generally but incorrectly assumed to be a right of way through to St Mary Street. Its owners were careful to close off the arcade on one day every year, thus preventing any claims that the public had access by right. Bon Marché (later incorporated into the Edwin Jones store chain) occupied the Clinton shops shown here, and when Edwin Jones eventually took over the whole building the arcade disappeared. The painted sign on the School Street wall of long-established local florist William Whittle's shop was a local 'landmark' for many years.

*St Thomas Street, 2003*

Today's view was taken from the same spot – a first-floor window at the northern end of Frederick Place – and changes in the street scene are minimal, although the ground floor of the former Clinton Arcade is currently two separate units: a Mothercare shop and the Bella Pasta restaurant. St Thomas Street was pedestrianised southward in 1989 beyond its junction with School Street, but buses continued to use the street until 2000, when they were rerouted to stops at the rear of Debenhams department store on Commercial Road, following the opening of the New Bond Street shopping centre. The wall of the building of the former William Whittle's flower shop now advertises the nearby Colwell Shopping Centre.

*'The Baths' in St Thomas Street dated from the 1840s and were demolished in 1926 to make way for the Clinton building. Here visitors and locals were able to sample the delights of hot and cold sea-water baths without actually venturing into the briny. This photograph from around 1860 shows the St Thomas Street entrance, and there was a similar handsome colonnaded façade in St Mary Street. The buildings beyond the baths can be readily identified in the 1954 and 2003 pictures. At 11 Frederick Place, opposite the baths, a commemorative plaque adorns the former home of the naturalist William Thompson (1822–79) – acknowledged as the first successful underwater photographer. This early photograph of the Baths was also taken by William Thompson.*

*Her Majesty Queen Elizabeth II, accompanied by Prince Charles, visited Weymouth in April 1959, en route to inspect HMS Eagle in Portland Harbour. When the Royal Train arrived at Weymouth Station, this bouquet of orchids, lilies and roses, arranged by florists at William Whittle, was presented to Her Majesty by five-year-old Grace Forder, daughter of the rector of Radipole.*

# Stottingway Street, Upwey

*Stottingway Street, c.1925*

This view of Stottingway Street at Upwey dates from the 1920s, and was taken from the Dorchester Road end of the street. Stottingway is an ancient place name and appears as early as 1212, then spelt 'Stottingwaie'. The rather superfluous addition of 'Street' is modern.

*Stottingway Street, 2003*

The scene in 2003 is still attractively rural. The wall on the right still exists, but the cottage in the foreground is now a ruin, with little left above ground level. The thatch of the roof of the adjacent cottage has been replaced by tiles but Stottingway, like most of Upwey village, retains much of the charm of an earlier age.

*Another photograph from the 1920s shows Stottingway Street at its junction with a traffic-free Dorchester Road. In the background on the right can be seen Upwey's Congregational Church, founded in 1802 when the Free Church movement began to expand out from the towns and build churches in the more rural areas. The church was rebuilt in 1880 and although it still stands, it was closed as a place of worship in 1992, having been known for its last twenty years as Upwey United Reformed Church.*

*At the other end of Stottingway can be found the attractive stone bridge which spans the River Wey and provides access to Upwey's historic Westbrook Manor. The weirs at the foot of Stottingway make this one of the prettiest sections of the river's 4-mile course to the sea.*

# Sutton Poyntz

*Sutton Poyntz, c.1925*

An idyllic scene at Sutton Poyntz in the 1920s, yet thirty years later the village would be described as a disgrace to the borough when a row of cottages to the right of the pond fell into a ruinous state and the pond itself was allowed to become overgrown and choked with weeds.

*Sutton Poyntz, 2003*

In 2002 the duckpond sparkles and several thatched cottages which by the 1950s had become too tumbledown to restore have been rebuilt in a style which suits the village scene. Truly a 'picture-postcard' view today. The barn in the background still stands, but no longer boasts a thatched roof.

*The Preston and Sutton Poyntz area has supplied water to the town (at first only to Melcombe Regis) for more than 200 years. In the early days the supply, from Boiling Rock, was by gravity and no pumping was required. This source eventually proving inadequate, the springs at Sutton Poyntz were acquired and the present pumping station built in 1856 by the Weymouth Waterworks Company, and later much extended. The original water-driven pumps gave way to steam in 1869, which in turn was replaced by the installation of electric pumps in 1958, the whole process being fully automated by the early 1980s. The tall chimney, which had been redundant for over twenty years, was taken down in 1979. Since 1934 an additional source of the water pumped to the town has been at Empool, West Knighton.*

*In 1859 Isambard Kingdom Brunel's favourite steamship, the Great Eastern, was due at Portland for coaling during her acceptance trials in the channel. She duly arrived, but only after a tragedy at sea which cost the lives of six of her crew. A tremendous explosion blew out her forward funnel and the six were scalded to death by the escaping steam. Here the huge vessel is seen at Portland, where a new funnel was constructed and installed. The ship proved to be something of a tourist attraction and the crowd on shore is awaiting the return of the paddle-steamer which ferried sightseers out to her where, for a fee, they could wander around the decks of Brunel's 'great babe', then the biggest vessel afloat. The discarded funnel from the Great Eastern was taken to Sutton Poyntz waterworks where it was installed in the ground as a vertical pipe through which millions of gallons of water have since flowed, and it is now one of the attractions at the Sutton Poyntz Water Supply Museum.*

# Town Bridge 1

*Town Bridge, 1928*

This 1928 view was taken shortly before the demolition men moved in to take down the 'old' Town Bridge which would be replaced by the present Town Bridge, opened in 1930. A number of bridges have spanned the harbour since the first was built to link Weymouth and Melcombe Regis in the 1590s, and the one pictured here was a substantial rebuild in the 1880s of the first stone bridge of 1824 (previous structures were largely of timber). Also to succumb to the demolition squad in 1928 were the bow-windowed shops and offices of the original Town Bridge Buildings on the right. On the left, Dennett the greengrocer and the Palladium Cinema occupied buildings still in use today. Across the Bridge, Holy Trinity Church consecrated in 1836 – a gift to the town from the Revd George Chamberlaine of Wyke Regis – provides a fine focal point, and the little spire to the right of the church belonged to Holy Trinity School at Chapelhay. The prominent hoardings advertise a review at the Regent Theatre which was not at the Town Bridge, but was located at the other end of St Thomas Street.

*Town Bridge, 2003*

Although much cluttered by road signs and street furniture, the scene in 2003 is still easily recognisable. The replacement Town Bridge Buildings are purely functional and lack the charm of those of yesteryear. Those on the left remain; Dennetts is now occupied by the Marlboro fish and chip restaurant and take-away, and the Palladium Cinema is now the Rendezvous café and nightclub. Many will remember this building during its years as Pankhurst's motorcycle showrooms.

*A charming engraving of the 1850s shows Holy Trinity School on the high ground at Chapelhay, behind the mother church. These little engravings some 3½ inches x 2½ inches in size were popular holiday souvenirs for visitors to take home before the advent of the picture postcard. Once the postcard industry got under way in the early 1900s and the craze for collecting picture postcards took off, photographers were out in force capturing local scenes and events for visitors to send home with the traditional message 'Wish you were here'.*

*Until quite late in the twentieth century the opening of the Town Bridge was quite an event, with due notice being given in the press that the bridge would be raised on certain dates. Now the numbers of pleasure craft mooring in the upper reaches of Weymouth Harbour and requiring access to the sea have brought about the introduction of a regular timetable of bridge opening. In summer every two hours during the main part of the day alarms sound and these barriers are lowered to warn pedestrians and traffic that the Town Bridge is about to be opened. Close to, the raised bridge is an impressive sight and usually draws a crowd of sightseers as well as those waiting to cross or pass on the waters below.*

# Town Bridge 2

*Town Bridge, 1914*

A view from the opposite direction to that of the previous 1928 picture, and of slightly earlier date – 1914.  The old Town Bridge Buildings are on the left and screen the lower end of St Thomas Street, including the Crown Hotel, from view.  In the centre stands Strong & Williams' ironmonger's shop.

*Town Bridge, 2003*

Taken in 2003 the most notable change is probably the Town Bridge itself, opened in July 1930 by the Duke of York (later King George VI). Town Bridge Buildings have been replaced, and it was when the present Town Bridge was being rebuilt that the Crown Hotel was much enlarged, the original Victorian building being surrounded by red-brick extensions. In 1937 a decision was taken to widen the lower end of St Thomas Street and it was in this year that the big shop of Strong & Williams was demolished – unnecessarily as it turned out, since St Thomas Street has not been much altered from this time. Other buildings in the street scene can still be identified today in this photograph taken almost ninety years after the one above it.

*This view of the raised bridge from water level dates from 1930 and is probably a trial lifting before the official opening on 4 July.*

*A second 1914 view, taken from the harbourside, shows the Town Bridge of 1880–1928 and the narrow arch under which ran the lines of the Weymouth Harbour Tramway. Steps then, as now, led down to the quayside from the bridge, although there was no wall along the water's edge to prevent the unsteady or unwary from falling into the harbour (note the lifebuoy beside the flight of steps).*

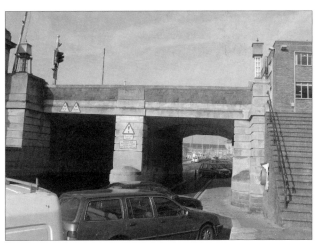

*The 1930 bridge seen from the same vantage point in 2003, showing how the quay has been widened to accommodate both a roadway and the railway line. Although superficially the same, the steps are not the original ones – as a count of the flight will show!*

# Upwey Mill

*Upwey Mill, c.1925*

A fine 1920s photograph of Upwey Mill on the River Wey, when the great water-wheel was turning and the mill buildings were alive with the clank of machinery and the splash of water as the miller produced Upwey flour. The huge mill dates from 1802 and scenes from Thomas Hardy's novel of the Napoleonic era *The Trumpet Major* are set in 'Overcombe Mill', which Hardy himself said contained features from both Upwey and Sutton Poyntz mills.

*Upwey Mill, 2003*

The Church Street scene in 2003 is as attractive now it was then.  Save for the new gates, little has changed in the eighty years which separate the two pictures.

*The mill was powered by water from the River Wey, the source of which is just above what is now Upwey Wishing Well.  The 'Wishing Well' name came into use after the publication of a novel by Hawley Smart in 1874.  The book, a romantic tale of adventure called* Broken Bonds, *was partly set beside the Springs at Upwey which Smart named the 'Wishing Well' and the new name was soon adopted locally.   This engraving of 'The Springs' predates the novel by more than eighty years, and was intended to be one of a second series of local views published by John Love, a Weymouth bookseller, but Love died in 1791 and the set was never completed.*

*Trips to the local beauty spots usually began at the King's Statue where wagonettes lined up ready to take passengers out and about.  Upwey Wishing Well was a favourite destination, where an afternoon visit could be rounded off with a cream tea at English's Tea Rooms before the ride back to Weymouth in the horse-drawn coach 'Vivid'.*

# Waterworks Company Offices, St Thomas Street

*Waterworks Company Offices, c.1920*

The offices of 'The Company of Proprietors of Weymouth Waterworks' were in this building on the corner of Bond Street and St Thomas Street until 1930, the company then moving to premises in Mitchell Street. The Waterworks Company had been founded in 1797 to bring water to the town from Boiling Rock at Preston. This source proving insufficient, a new supply was piped to the town from Sutton Poyntz in the 1850s, supplemented in 1934 by water from the springs at West Knighton. In 1969 the formerly independent company joined others to form the Dorset Water Board, and in 1974 became part of the Wessex Water Authority.

*Waterworks Company Offices, 2003*

Once the Water Company had left St Thomas Street the premises were taken over for retail use and a variety of furnishing shops were here between the 1930s and 1990s. S. Thomas (Ideal Homes) was followed by Jays, then Woodhouse and finally, Times Furnishing. Plans to redevelop this corner as part of a new shopping precinct were very slow in coming to fruition and properties on the north side of Lower Bond Street, including this corner site, lay empty and boarded up, becoming more dilapidated and vandalised with every month that passed. Eventually the new shopping precinct took shape and 'New Bond Street' in 2000 opened as an attractive town square of department stores and smaller shops. The old Water Company building was rebuilt as the New Look store, a clothing company which began its life in Weymouth and now has its main offices and distribution centre in Mercery Road at Radipole. The new shop echoes in one respect the architecture of its predecessor on the site, as both Water Company offices and the New Look shop feature a corner 'tower' above their entrances.

*By the 1980s Woodhouse Furnishers had moved into the former Water Company offices at 77 St Thomas Street. Once the building was taken over by the retail trade it was inevitable that plate-glass windows would be installed at street level, and these were attractive, with decorative art deco panels at the top. Otherwise No. 77 had changed little, apart from the removal of a chimney and gable on the Lower Bond Street façade. The gentleman passing the Woodhouse shop in the early 1980s is rather unusually attired in the drape jacket and drainpipe trousers of the earlier 'Teddy Boy' era of the 1950s. This is 'Jumping Jimmy Thunder', a well-known local Elvis Presley impersonator and pub act, probably making his way to perform at the 'Golden Eagle' pub in Lower Bond Street.*

*Traffic delays on Dorchester Road caused by burst water mains had long been a regular feature in the lives of drivers commuting to Dorchester. In 2002 Wessex Water announced that to overcome the problem the old water supply pipes would be replaced along the whole of the stretch of road between the Manor Road roundabout and Broadwey. Work began in October 2002 resulting inevitably in months of traffic queues as the road works restricted vehicles section by section to a single lane, as seen here. At time of writing in April 2003 the works were nearing completion, promising an end to a longstanding problem.*

*In the 1890s springs at Upwey began supplying water to Portland, with the original pumping works being at Gould's Hill, but by the early 1900s the source was proving inadequate for the island's increasing demand. This pumping station at Friar Waddon, opened in January 1914, became Portland's new supplier.*

# Westerhall

*Westerhall, 1870s*

A rather tranquil scene at Westerhall (more correctly, Westerhall Road) in the 1870s, as the development of this stretch of road linking Dorchester Road and Greenhill began. The houses on the left – Westerhall Villas – have not been long built and trees in front of them are newly planted. Perhaps this road was planned as a quiet avenue! The large building in the background on the right is Weymouth College, the boys' public school. It had been founded in the early 1860s in what is now the Arts Centre in Commercial Road, moving to the Dorchester Road site in 1864. Westerhall is built on land of the Johnstone Estate, owned at this time by Sir Frederic Johnstone of Westerhall in Dumfriesshire, hence its name. Sir Frederic was Tory MP for the town at the same time as Henry Edwards, who represented the Liberals.

*Westerhall, 2003*

Normally, traffic constantly sweeps past Westerhall's houses, as the one-way system here routes vehicles into lanes for town or the Preston Road – so we had to linger for quite a while to get this car-free shot to reveal the changes in the background. One problem was the number of courteous motorists who pulled up, thinking that we were just waiting to cross the road! The houses, apart from conversion to hotel use, are not greatly changed and Morven House and St Helen's (centre, left) retain the crossed timbers which decorate the eaves in the earlier picture. The empty land on the right of the 1870 photograph was filled with houses early in the twentieth century and some of these have since been replaced with more modern apartment blocks. Today the build-up of housing here and along Dorchester Road has obscured the College building from view.

In the foreground, on the left, and much extended since it was first built, is the Province of Natal Hotel. Formerly the Grosvenor Hotel. It reopened as the Royal Naval Hotel in May 1949, managed by the British Sailors' Society and purchased for the Navy by King George's Fund for Sailors, with money raised by the people of Natal in a 'Salute to Britain' fund. The hotel provided holiday accommodation for the families of Royal Navy personnel serving at Portland. When the RN presence in the area declined, the hotel went over to civilian use, but its name maintains the South African link.

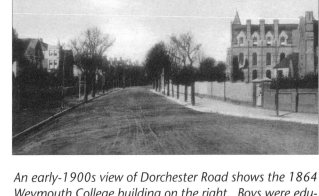

*An early-1900s view of Dorchester Road shows the 1864 Weymouth College building on the right. Boys were educated at the public school until early in 1940 when, because of hostilities, the school closed and its students transferred to Wellingborough, Northants. After various wartime uses, the buildings were taken over and later extended by Weymouth Teacher Training College, which in turn became part of the Dorset Institute of Higher Education. Today the site is again occupied by Weymouth College – but this is a twentieth-century tertiary college, which adopted the old school's name. The modern College has erected extensive new buildings and, after being used for educational purposes for almost 150 years, the Victorian building was no longer required and is being converted to housing.*

*These gardens at the end of St John's Terrace were laid out as a shrubbery in 1904 on land given by Sir Frederic Johnstone. The St John's Gardens were later planted with roses and are today a quiet spot to the north of the Esplanade, where road lanes channel today's busy traffic towards Dorchester or Wareham as it leaves the town.*

# Westham Bridge

*Westham Bridge, 1950s*

This 1950s view taken from the Melcombe side of Westham Bridge shows
(centre) the Health Centre in Abbotsbury Road, a building which opened
on the same day as Weymouth Town Bridge – 4 July 1930. To the right is

the terminus of the Miniature Railway, well sited to attract the hundreds of visitors who poured out of the coaches using the adjacent Westham Coach Park during the summer season. The little steam trains ran along the western shore of Radipole Lake. St Joseph's Roman Catholic Church, on the left, had been built in 1934.

*Wetsham Bridge, 2003*

In the 2003 picture Westham Bridge is the feature least changed in fifty years, although today it is not possible to drive across the bridge which is currently used only as a car park. On the left, apartment blocks, to be known as Harbour View, are under construction on a site on which stood, until 1990, the prefabricated buildings of the old Weymouth Public Library. The Health Centre was demolished in 2002, and when this photograph was taken the foundations of another apartment block were already taking its place. When the flats are completed, this view looking up Abbotsbury Road towards Westham will be lost for ever. Additionally, 1980s road improvements and the construction of a large traffic island have completely altered the far shore where the miniature railway once ran.

*The little steam railway at Westham Coach Park opened in June 1947, and was operated by Messrs David Curwen Ltd. of Baydon, Marlborough. The loco is a scale model of the LNER A 2/1 Pacific, and its average speed along the quarter-mile (400m) of track along the lake shore was around 20 mph (32 kph), pulling six coaches with a capacity load of 72 passengers.*

*The Westham Health Centre viewed from Westwey Road shortly before demolition in 2002, with the former town ambulance station – predating the one in Westwey Road – clearly visible on its right-hand side.*

# Westham Road

*Westham Road, 1938*

Prior to 1938 the south side of Westham Road (once known as Little George Street) consisted of a nineteenth-century terrace of mansard-roofed, bow-windowed houses with small shops at street level. Houses of this design appear in several areas of the town. The large building beyond them was then a dairy run by Mrs Jeffrey and the 'Jeffrey's Dairy' name was to remain through several ownerships. On the corner of Frederick Place, at the top end of St Thomas Street, was Forte's Café and this was always known as Forte's Corner (and probably will continue to be so called by the generations of Weymouthians who drank coffee, enjoyed Knickerbocker Glory sundaes, queued outside for ice-creams and used the corner as a meeting place).

*Westham Road, 2003*

The terrace houses were pulled down in 1938 to make way for road widening and the building of the present shops on this site: functional, but lacking the charm of the earlier properties. Jeffrey's Dairy is now occupied by the Lunch Box, a take-away and café, having been owned by Piggott's DIY store in the late 1970s and 1980s, and when Forte's closed the Hogshead pub chain took over the premises at the top end of St Thomas Street.

*A close-up view of the typical 'Weymouth-style' early-nineteenth-century terrace houses, seen here at the corner of Great George Street and Westham Road before the 1930s redevelopment. Crosby's is now occupied by Williams the Baker. Millers Sausages' delivery van is parked outside Monkton Dairies, today an Indian take-away.*

*The Manor Café was behind Vaux's baker's shop in Westham Road. Tea taken here, with a mouthwatering cream cake, was a delight.*

*A little before the old Westham Road shops were taken down, the roadway at the top of Westham Road had been widened by the demolition of the end house of Royal Terrace. The corner was reconstructed in typical 1930s style, with the Southern Electricity Board occupying new ground floor showrooms (currently The Cookshop). Visible today on the upper outside wall is this attractive stonework sunburst, which still has traces of its original gilding.*

# Westwey Road

*Westwey Road, c.1935*

Looking along Westwey Road towards the Westham area of Weymouth, this mid-1930s photograph shows an industrial scene along the western shore of the Inner Harbour, or Backwater, where the town's gas and electricity supplies were generated. At this date, the harbour wall and

Westwey Road were both relatively new structures which had followed as a result of major land reclamation. The vessel shown is the London-registered *Lido*, a regular visitor to the port collecting tar, a regular by-product of the gas industry, which was pumped to the tar-boat through a pipe under Westwey Road. She was built in 1926 at Faversham in Kent and at the time of the photograph was in the ownership of the Union Lighterage Company. Powered by a single Gardner diesel engine, the *Lido* was 92ft (28m) long and had a gross weight of 160 tons.

*Westwey Road, 2003*

Since 1972 Westwey House, the local office of the Benefits Agency, has occupied the former gasworks site, which was cleared in the early 1960s, although a gasometer erected in the 1950s remains in use. Westwey House was extensively modernised in the 1990s. The houses in Stavordale Road, which are visible in the background of the earlier picture, are obscured by the flat-roofed Magistrates' Court of 1978.

*This comprehensive aerial photograph shows just how much industry occupied the land between the railway embankment of the Weymouth and Portland Railway and the Inner Harbour. Railway, gasworks and the electricity power station are shown, and the Borough Council yard and workshops were close to Westham Bridge. Most interesting of all in this late-1920s shot is that Westwey Road did not exist at all. The extensive reclamation to extend the gasworks site and build Westwey Road had not yet begun and it was not until 1932 that the new road was opened to traffic. The train is crossing the Newstead Road overbridge, which was demolished in 1987.*

*Located at the southern end of Westwey Road, at the foot of Boot Hill, the Sidney Hall opened in 1900 and was a gift to Holy Trinity parish from Sir John Groves, of the Hope Square brewery. It was intended for the use of the Church Lads' Brigade, and is named in memory of Sir John's son Sidney, a lieutenant in the Church Lads' Brigade who also served in the Dorset Rifle Volunteers and died, aged twenty-six, in 1895. When first built, the hall was fitted out in military style and its accommodation included a drill hall and armoury. Weymouth residents later in the twentieth century will recall hectic roller skating sessions at the Sidney Hall, whilst in its latter days it went over to bingo.*

# Weymouth and District Hospital

*Weymouth and District Hospital, c.1925*

Weymouth and District Hospital, then known as the Princess Christian Hospital and Sanatorium, opened on 19 November 1902 in a new avenue off Westerhall Road, known then as Bent Path Avenue, but today as Melcombe Avenue. The institution, founded in 1848 as the Weymouth Sanatorium, had originally been located in the town centre and from the 1860s was in Clarence Buildings, close to the harbourside. With the constant din from ship repair yards, cargo loading and unloading, and the early embarkation of passengers leaving on the Channel

Islands vessels – boats left at 6am on Mondays, Wednesdays and Fridays – this was not the ideal location for patients requiring peace and quiet. The new site at Greenhill was thought to be 'a very healthy one, open to the sea breezes, standing high up, with good views and a south-east aspect and surrounded by tastefully laid out grounds'. Local firm Crickmay & Sons, designers of innumerable buildings in and around Weymouth, were the architects of the new hospital and the driving force behind the project was Dr James Macpherson Lawrie. In 1921 the Royal Hospital in School Street merged with the Princess Christian Hospital and the Melcombe Avenue building took on the once familiar name Weymouth and District Hospital. Inevitably, as the years passed, the hospital outgrew its original premises and various extensions were added to it, but this photograph of the 1920s shows it as originally built.

*Weymouth and District Hospital, 2003*

Today nothing remains of the building hailed in 1902 as 'the latest and most approved hospital type'. On the completion of the Dorset County Hospital at Dorchester in May 1998 the majority of in-patients were transferred to the new hospital and Weymouth and District Hospital gradually shut down. Today it is only extensions to the 1902 building which remain in use as Weymouth Community Hospital, a Small Accident and Injuries Unit, with various out-patient facilities and wards for the care of the elderly. The original building shown in the old picture was demolished early in 1999, and the empty space on which it once stood is now being used as the car park for those visiting the hospital.

*One week before D-Day, as craft of the invasion force were assembling in Weymouth Bay and Portland Harbour, the town suffered what was to be its last air raid of the war, a sharp and vicious night-time attack in which Weymouth and District Hospital and houses in Melcombe Avenue were hit, with one bomb destroying the hospital's out-patients department. As rescue workers hastened to the scene, three ARP men from the depot in Cranford Avenue were killed as more bombs fell. Patients from the Hospital were swiftly evacuated to nearby Weymouth College, serving as an emergency hospital.*

*An estimated total of 19 bombs fell on the town that night. In addition to the damage to the hospital and houses in Melcombe Avenue, the Christian Science Church was ablaze, water mains were out of action, one bomb made a huge crater some 30 feet (9.1m) deep in Lynmoor Road, and the Weymouth and Dorset County Eye Infirmary at Greenhill had all its windows blown in. Stretcher bearers of the U.S. Army Medical Services assisted at the scene, which was close to Dorchester Road where great convoys of American troops and vehicles would soon be due to pass en route for D-Day embarkation at Weymouth and Portland harbours. Of great concern, therefore, was the location of a deeply buried unexploded bomb in Melcombe Avenue, and a bomb disposal team under Lieutenant R.A.J Woods was called in to deal with the situation. Work started on Sunday 28 May, the day of the raid, and continued until the early hours of Friday 3 June when the bomb was successfully defused and removed – to the relief of all! Lieutenant Woods was later awarded the George Medal for his war work as Dorset's Bomb Disposal Officer. The photograph shows the Police Liaison Officer, Inspector Martyn, with the defused bomb.*

*Weymouth Community Hospital in 2003, seen from Westerhall's junction with Dorchester Road. With the resort's population rising to over 150,000 during the summer season, the Small Accident and Injuries Unit can, at times, be very busy!*

# Weymouth Lifeboat

*Weymouth Lifeboat, c.1910*

A dramatic shot of the launch of the lifeboat around 1910, the boat being the *Friern Watch*, in service at Weymouth from 1903 until 1924. This was the second vessel stationed at Weymouth bearing this unusual name. It was derived from the name of a house – formerly the watch-gate to a friary – which belonged to the donor of both lifeboats, a Mr E. Homan.

Then, as now, the lifeboat house was on Nothe Parade, although it was much enlarged in 1903 and, again, in 1924. These spectacular slipway launches had ceased by 1930 when the *William and Clara Ryland* arrived on station and was kept afloat in the harbour.

*Weymouth Lifeboat, 2003*

One of the busiest RNLI vessels in the British Isles, today the lifeboat lies afloat outside the lifeboat house, ready for her next call to action. In 2003 the lifeboat, the Weymouth station's ninth, is the *Ernest and Mabel* named after the parents of the prime donor Miss Beryl Taylor. The naming ceremony took place on 14 September 2002. The lifeboat is a Severn Class vessel, with a top speed of 25 knots and carrying the numbers '17 – 32' on her hull, indicating her length of 17 metres and that she is the 32nd vessel of this class to enter service. Weymouth has a second lifeboat, an Atlantic 75B Class inshore rescue boat – *Phyl Clare III* – which is kept ashore and launched from the former Cosens slipway a little nearer the harbour mouth.

*A very familiar sight in the harbour for more than twenty-five years and one remembered by many Weymouthians was the lifeboat* William and Clara Ryland, *a 51ft Barnett class motor lifeboat, built at Cowes, Isle of Wight and paid for by the legacy of William Ryland of Sheffield. She served at Weymouth from 1930 until 1957, being replaced by the* Frank Spiller Locke *and, in 1974, by the* Tony Vandervell. *The picture has something of an air of celebration about it, and this may have been one of the traditional Christmas trips to visit the crew of the Shambles Lightship. Today such visits are no longer necessary, as the hazards of the Shambles Bank, east of Portland Bill, have been marked by an automatic buoy since 1973.*

*Based at the former Naval Air Station at Portland, which closed in March 1999, and under contract to HM Coastguard, Bristow Helicopters operate the Sikorsky S-61N in the search and rescue role – co-operating closely with the Weymouth lifeboats and other emergency services. Here we see G-BPWB exercising in Portland Harbour, with the coastline between the Bincleaves Breakwater and Sandsfoot Castle in the background.*

# Weymouth Sands

*Weymouth Sands, c.1900*

All the fun of the seaside in a beach scene of around 1900 with children in the foreground enjoying donkey rides. Other donkeys behind them tuck into a trough of hay, and goats wait patiently beside their carriages below the Esplanade wall. A short trip in a wickerwork cart or one of the miniature landaus pulled by goats was a popular alternative to the traditional ride on a donkey. Holiday souvenir photographs could be taken at the American Studio and on the right children queue at the ice-cream cart. The office of the Weymouth Bathing Machines and Saloons is in the centre of the photograph and the big octagonal machines on the sands date from the Georgian period. These were hired individually; the saloons, at the water's edge and out of sight in this photograph, consisted of a series of cubicles in one much larger machine and were cheaper. The Gentlemen's Saloon and the Ladies' Saloon were kept a regulation distance apart as no mixed bathing was permitted at Weymouth until 1908, but it was introduced here several years before it was allowed at resorts such as Blackpool and Scarborough. The big Royal Hotel had not been long in business when this picture was taken, having opened in 1897, six years after the first Georgian Royal Hotel was pulled down. Initial schemes for a new 'Royal' were cash strapped and the razed site was an untidy gap in the middle of the Esplanade for several years.

*Weymouth Sands, 2003*

What a difference a little sunshine makes! Although taken on a June afternoon in 2003, the beach was virtually deserted under overcast skies and the few early-season holidaymakers who were about were seeking refuge in the Victorian Esplanade shelters from a chilly sea breeze. Today the bathing machines office has its place taken by a stripy refreshment kiosk, one of several which appear on the beach for the summer season. Note, to the left of the picture, the Land Train 'awaiting the off' for its trip along the Esplanade to Greenhill Gardens and Sealife Centre on Preston Beach Road. Unusually, and as can be seen, one of the Georgian terraced houses next to the Royal Hotel was much altered in the twentieth century and now sports a striking art deco façade.

*Chambers' photographers patrolled the Esplanade and sands from the late 1940s, taking pictures which could be collected from their kiosk later, and thousands of their prints must exist in family albums. This one was taken near the Tea Cabin, but there are few clues to the identity of the lady and little boy. On the reverse is written 'Mummie on her 60th birthday at Weymouth. Graham age 3 yrs 5 months and 2 weeks'.*

*Another sea-front scene, this one from the 1930s when the first 'Concours d'Elegance' motor rally, described as 'a beauty parade of cars', was held on the Esplanade in September 1934. The cars, of course, are the stars, and many names from the past are represented in the line-up – Lagonda, Talbot, Humber, Alvis and Armstrong-Siddeley – as well as others still producing ranges today such as Rolls Royce and Vauxhall. Cup for the best-kept and smartest trade car owned and run by a Weymouth tradesman went to Hallett & Son, local furnishers, for their 26-horsepower Bedford which is at the end of the line-up. A smartly uniformed RAC (or is he AA?) patrolman makes his way along the prom as crowds inspect the vehicles. On the beach can be seen the open-air Vaudeville Theatre where concert parties entertained during the season.*

# Whitehead's Torpedo Factory, Ferrybridge

*Whitehead's Torpedo Factory, c.1900*

Industry came to Wyke Regis in 1891 with the opening of the Whitehead's Torpedo Factory at Ferrybridge and, as can be seen, the factory had its own siding off the Weymouth and Portland Railway. The 'old' village of Wyke, which had grown up around the church and Square, was some distance from the new factory, which employed a considerable workforce. As a result the developments along Portland Road began, with houses in the streets branching off it largely occupied by Whitehead's employees. Gallwey Road is named after the factory's first manager, Captain Payne Gallwey, and the first school in Victoria Road (now replaced by newer buildings) was built by the company. It was to be some time before Wyke Halt, close to Whitehead's, opened in 1909, much more a station for the factory workers than for the village, from which it was a considerable distance.

*Whitehead's Torpedo Factory, 2003*

In 2003 practically all trace of Whitehead's Torpedo Factory has disappeared, as has the adjacent Weymouth and Portland Railway. This photograph was taken beside the now tarmacked line of the Rodwell Trail, which follows the route of the old railway from Westham to Wyke Regis. The factory buildings were demolished in 1997 and these houses of 'Harbour Point' now fill the site.

*A view of the factory buildings from Smallmouth, taken in the late 1960s. Whitehead's delivered its last torpedo for the Royal Navy from its wartime contract in 1946, but work on similar projects continued until 1966, when the very last torpedo trial was conducted in nearby Portland Harbour. The company's successors on the site were Vickers-Armstrong, Wellworthy and finally A.E. Piston Products.*

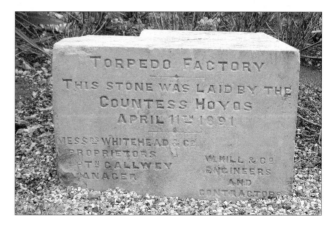

*A little bit of Whitehead's history has been preserved amongst the modern houses – the original foundation stone of the torpedo works, laid in April 1891 by the Countess Hoyos, daughter of the torpedo's inventor, Robert Whitehead. Commemorative tablets have also been placed in the centre of the new development, detailing the site's importance in the history of Wyke Regis.*

# Wyke Regis Memorial Hall

*Wyke Regis Parish Room, c.1905*

The Parish Room at Wyke Regis started life as the first school in the village to be part funded by the Government. Previously classes had been held by the parish priest and by a lady who ran a Dame School, neither being properly able to cater for the growing number of children in the community. This 'National School' opened in 1858 to provide elementary education for poor children in the parish. By the 1890s it was becoming overcrowded and in 1897 larger school buildings opened in Victoria Road, paid for by the Whitehead's Torpedo Company. This scene looks up Chamberlaine Road (on the right) towards Portland Road.

*Wyke Regis Memorial Hall, 2003*

Late in 1908 a new building – the Memorial Hall – was dedicated on the site of the old Parish Room. This well-used community facility was built in memory of Margaret, wife of the Revd George Chamberlaine, rector of Wyke Regis 1809–37. The trust that he set up which provided the hall was one of a number of his charitable acts for the benefit of the parish, the best known being the construction of Holy Trinity Church in Weymouth, paid for at his sole expense. In 1988 the village of Wyke Regis held grand celebrations to commemorate its one thousand years of recorded history and a plaque in the wall of the Memorial Hall records this historic event, the first mention of Wyke being in a charter of 988.

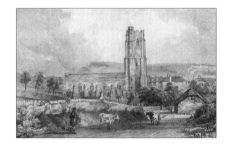

*The tower of the parish church of All Saints' appears in both photographs opposite. Consecrated in 1455, it was built on the site of an earlier church. All Saints' was the mother church for the people of Weymouth, who, although they had a chapel of ease at Chapelhay in medieval times, were to have no parish church of their own until Holy Trinity was built beside the Town Bridge in 1836.*